FREDERICK TRENCH (1746–1836)
AND HEYWOOD, QUEEN'S COUNTY

T0167589

Maynooth Studies in Irish Local History

SERIES EDITOR Raymond Gillespie

This is one of six new pamphlets in the Maynooth Studies in Irish Local History Series to be published in the year 2000. Like their predecessors, most of the pamphlets are based on theses completed as part of the M.A. in local history programme in National University of Ireland, Maynooth. While the regions and time span which they cover are diverse, from Waterford to Monaghan, and from the fourteenth to the twentieth centuries, they all share a conviction that the exploration of the local past can shed light on the evolution of modern societies. They each demonstrate that understanding the evolution of local societies is important. The local worlds of Ireland in the past are as complex and sophisticated as the national framework in which they are set. The communities which peopled those local worlds, whether they be the inhabitants of religious houses, industrial villages or rural parishes, shaped and were shaped by their environments to create a series of interlocking worlds of considerable complexity. Those past worlds are best interpreted not through local administrative divisions, such as the county, but in human units: local places where communities of people lived and died. Untangling what held these communities together, and what drove them apart, gives us new insights into the world we have lost.

These pamphlets each make a significant contribution to understanding Irish society in the past. Together with twenty-eight earlier works in this series they explore something of the hopes and fears of those who lived in Irish local communities in the past. In doing so they provide examples of the practice of local history at its best and show the vibrant discipline which the study of local history in Ireland has become in recent years.

Maynooth Studies in Irish Local History: Number 32

Frederick Trench, 1746–1836 and Heywood, Queen's County:
the creation of a romantic landscape

Patricia Friel

IRISH ACADEMIC PRESS
DUBLIN • PORTLAND, OR

First published in 2000 by
IRISH ACADEMIC PRESS
44, Northumberland Road, Dublin 4, Ireland
and in the United States of America by
IRISH ACADEMIC PRESS
c/o ISBS, 5804 NE Hassalo Street, Portland, OR 97213–3644.

website: www.iap.ie

© Patricia Friel 2000

British Library Cataloguing in Publication Data
Friel, Patricia
    Frederick Trench, 1746–1836 and Heywood, Queen's County : the creation of a
romantic landscape. – (Maynooth studies in Irish local history; no. 32)
    1. Trench, Frederick 2. Gentry – Ireland – Biography 3. Ballinakill (Ireland) –
History – 19th century
    I. Title
    941.8'7'081'092

    ISBN 0–7165–2721–9

Library of Congress Cataloging-in-Publication Data
Friel, Patricia.
    Frederick Trench, 1746–1836 and Heywood, Queen's County : the creation of a
romantic landscape / Patricia Friel.
      p. cm.—(Maynooth studies in local history ; no. 32)
    Based on the author's thesis (M.A.)—National University of Ireland, Maynooth.
    Includes bibliographical references.
    ISBN 0–7165–2721–9 (pb : alk. paper)
      1. Heywood Garden (Ireland)—History.   2. Trench, Frederick, 1746–1836—
Homes and haunts—Ireland—Laois—History.   3. Follies (Architecture)—
Ireland—Laois. I. Title. II. Series.
    SB466.I653 H494 2000
    712'.6'094187—dc21   00–044837

All rights reserved. Without limiting the rights under copyright reserved alone,
no part of this publication may be reproduced, stored in or introduced into a
retrieval system, or transmitted, in any form or by any means (electronic,
mechanical, photocopying, recording or otherwise), without the prior
written permission of both the copyright owner and the above
publisher of this book.

Typeset in 10 pt on 12 pt Bembo by
Carrigboy Typesetting Services, County Cork
Printed by ColourBooks Ltd., Dublin

Contents

ILLUSTRATIONS

Illustrations are from the following collections:
Figure 1: based on Samuel Lewis, *Atlas of Ireland* (London 1837).
Figure 2: from John Feehan and Christopher O'Shea,
      Aspects of local history, (Pallaskenry, undated).
Figure 3: based on K.A.O., U1590, P49.
Figure 4: based on 1838 Ordnance Survey, Queen's County, sheet 30, revised
      1906.
Figure 5: National Gallery of Ireland.
Figure 6: Courtauld Institute of Art.
Figures 7–11: Kilkenny Castle collection.

Acknowledgements

This paper is based on the thesis of my M.A. in Local History. For all their help and support over the period of that study, I would like to thank firstly the staff of the following institutions: N.U.I. Maynooth libraries (Maynooth and Kilkenny campuses), the National Library of Ireland, the Irish Architectural Archive, the National Archives, the National Gallery of Ireland, the Kent Archive Office (U.K.), Laois County Library, the Office of Public Works and Dúchas the Heritage Service. I would like to thank Dr. Jane Fenlon for her particular help, and Jane Meredith for sharing her work on Andrew Caldwell so generously. I would like to thank Dr. Raymond Gillespie for a great two years which I enjoyed enormously, and John Bradley for his help with this thesis. I would particularly like to thank my work colleagues for their patience while I was at this study, and finally Mary Burke and especially my children Owen Ardill and Chrissie Ardill for supporting me always.

Introduction

In 1994 fifty acres of land in Ballinakill, County Laois, were handed over by the Salesian Brothers to Dúchas, the heritage service of the Department of Arts, Heritage, Gaeltacht and the Islands, the state agency responsible for the preservation of such historic properties. Like many other religious orders at that time, having acquired the house and property from the Land Commission under the 1923 Land Act, the Salesians had had a seminary and school there in Heywood House. When the house accidentally burned down in 1950, the school had been rebuilt further back from the original site. By the 1990s, in keeping with Department of Education policy, that school was amalgamated with two other local schools to form the new Heywood Community School. At that point the Salesians transferred the school property to the Department of Education and the remaining fifty acres of their land to Dúchas.

These Heywood lands came under local Kilkenny management, and it was in trying to study and understand precisely what Dúchas had been given – in order to determine how it should be best managed – the realisation grew that there was much about the earlier landscape there, with its series of artificial lakes, follies and other buildings, which demanded a detailed study. So this study was undertaken in order to understand how the demesne estate of Heywood had come about and what it contained. This necessitated a study of how the Trench family, whose home Heywood had been, had come to Ballinakill, how they acquired the land there, what inspired Frederick Trench (1746–1836) to create the beautiful romantic landscape there and then how it had been physically made.

Heywood is relatively little known nowadays. Set in a remote corner of County Laois, it has slipped into a limbo of lost gardens, of forgotten worlds. While one can argue that it holds its own with any other romantic landscape in this country, if not the British Isles, it is seldom remembered at that level. Other landscape creations – more usually of the nobility – are well known, such as Carton, the Casino at Marino, Westport House or the Killarney properties, but somehow Heywood has been forgotten. When it was created in the last quarter of the eighteenth century Frederick Trench entertained and corresponded with such connoisseurs as Lords Charlemont and Charleville. But while their creations are well documented and visited, Heywood is not.

One brief but efficient description of Heywood is in Edward Malins and the Knight of Glin's excellent 1976 publication, *Lost Demesnes: Irish Landscape Gardening 1660–1845*. This book gives a very accomplished tour through the various trends in Irish gardens of its period, and describes Heywood as 'less grand but more elegant'[1] than Curraghmore County Waterford and gives a brief listing and illustration of the various elements of its landscape, before finishing 'Before Frederick Trench died (1836), this landscape in the Stourhead Romantic-poetic tradition, was perfect.'[2] While accurate in the facts it gives, this type of publication cannot do more than give a brief outline description of any property it includes and so there is much about Heywood it omits, many of the features of its landscape, and almost nothing about the background to the demesne.

The other publication important in any study of Irish landscape gardens is James Howley's *The Follies and Garden Buildings of Ireland*, (London 1993). This is a much more detailed study of the architectural heritage of Ireland's eighteenth-century gardens. Howley gives a comprehensive listing of all types of garden follies found throughout Ireland, and he very carefully describes many of the landscape buildings in Heywood. He is more concerned, however, with the actual buildings and thus can give only outline background or historical information for any property. He also describes follies by type, and of course there can be several different types within one garden.

In order to fully comprehend Heywood, it is important to understand it in different ways; its local position in both geographical and political terms, its physical landscape, how the Trench family came to be there and then why and how one particular member of that family, Frederick Trench (1746–1836) came to develop that landscape in that place. To do this required a consideration of the background to the Ballinakill area, the history of the Trench family and its relationship with Lord Stanhope, the owner of the land, of Frederick Trench himself – his interests and what prompted and influenced him to develop and build the demesne, of Trench's life, his family, his local community and how he worked with them to execute his vision for Heywood, and the landscape buildings themselves.

To date no study has been done on the development and subsequent decline of the plantation town of Ballinakill through the seventeenth, eighteenth and nineteenth centuries. In *Laois, an environmental history*,[3] John Feehan gives a good general background to the plantation town. To understand the background to the Queen's County of the time, a number of different sources were used. Arthur Young's account of his tours in 1776, 1777 and 1778[4] gave background information. This was the period of those great statistical surveys instigated by the Dublin Society, and Sir Charles Coote's 1801 survey of Queen's County[5] was very useful for contemporary details of Ballinakill and its society. For detailed information about Ballinakill itself there are the Stanhope papers (now in the Kent Archive Office) which contain very extensive material on this Irish estate, in particular much relevant estate correspondence and rentals. The other side of that particular landlord/tenant coin was in the Domvile papers in the National Library, which hold all the Trench material, including extensive material from Frederick Trench's time. Understandably, most of this material is in the form of letters received by Frederick Trench, rather than those he wrote. Here, in order to fill out this knowledge, I was very fortunate to join with Jane Meredith, who is studying Trench's close friend, Andrew Caldwell. Her generosity in sharing her research enabled me to fill in many gaps.

To understand Frederick Trench's interests it was also necessary to consider his life outside Ballinakill, particularly his life in Dublin, where he was one of that close group of friends who were all members of the Dublin Wide Streets Commissioners and supporters of the architect James Gandon. Here Edward McParland's detailed work provided much information on that society.[6] Frederick Trench's role in developing the Rotunda Gardens and in building the Assembly Rooms was based on a detailed study by Noreen Casey.[7] The biography of James Gandon[8] helped to give added colour to this picture.

It is important to bear in mind, too, that the late eighteenth century – and the particular romantic landscape in Heywood – was very much a visual world. It was designed to be viewed, walked through, observed, and appreciated. There are many illustrations of the family and very many of the grounds, a small sample of which are included here. These were done by all the leading Irish artists of the day including Malton, Comerford, Hamilton and Brocas, entirely in keeping with Frederick Trench's status, his style and taste.

By piecing all these elements together, a much clearer understanding of what Heywood was begins to emerge, of the society to which it belonged and how it came into being. Such romantic landscapes are infinitely delicate worlds and are nowadays at the mercy of modern agricultural practice and the persistent demand for lands for housing. While this study was being pursued, planning permission was granted by Laois County Council to build nineteen houses in the open field which contains the classical arch 'Claude's Seat', and which runs down to the lowest lake of Heywood. Based on this study of the historic landscape, Dúchas appealed the planning approval to An Bord Pleanála, and the appeal was upheld. This is the first time an appeal of this type has been upheld and it sets an important precedent in that it recognises that such landscapes are to be valued and respected even after two hundred years. It is also true that, without this study, the case for its preservation could not have had such a compelling factual base. This gives the study a value over and above its contribution to pure research and argues that as such work is done on different aspects of our history, it is absorbed into and influences how we view and, more importantly in this context, value our past.

Ballinakill, Queen's County and the Trench family

W hat we call Heywood Demesne today is what remains of a small estate of just over 250 acres at Ballinakill, County Laois, formerly called Queen's County (figure 1), which the Trench family rented from the owner, Lord Stanhope, throughout the eighteenth and nineteenth centuries. This is the parish of Dysart Gallen, later the barony of Cullenagh, on the edge of the Castlecomer hills which run between the modern counties of Kilkenny and Laois. Averaging five hundred feet above sea level, it is largely a shale and limestone area with large gravel deposits, resulting in gently rolling hills with many springs and streams, an area once described as 'Gallen of the pleasant streams'.[1]

This area of County Laois was traditionally O'More territory and in an inquisition taken at Maryborough in 1577[2] Dysart Gallen was listed as part of the territory of Rory O'More. The old church of Dysart Gallen – traditionally associated with Saint Manchan the Wise – is approximately three miles outside Ballinakill, and was described in 1870 thus:

> In a lovely and sheltered valley, through which a rushing and mountain stream rolls, beside this river the triangular-shaped graveyard of Disert-Gallen rises on a knoll. The situation is a lonely one, but the surrounding scenery for romantic beauty cannot be surpassed. Ash and other tall trees grew around the old graveyard and sheltered the church ruins, which rose in its midst.[3]

Following the English plantations of Laois and Offaly in 1606 Sir Thomas Coatch, proprietor of the Manor of Galline, was granted weekly markets and fairs in Ballinakill,[4] but it was his successor, Sir Thomas Ridgeway, earl of Londonderry, who planted an English colony there, built a castle for its protection and called his settlement Gallen-Ridgeway. To encourage its development the borough of Ballinakill was incorporated by charter by King James I in 1612, setting out arrangements for its corporation and freemen, for courts, markets, fairs and tolls, making it the only market town in the barony, and giving it the right to return two members to parliament.[5] In 1631 the manor of Gallen-Ridgway was described as having a large mansion or castle, one hundred messuages, a dovecot, two watermills, a fulling-mill, an iron-mill, courts leet and baron, three fairs and two markets.[6]

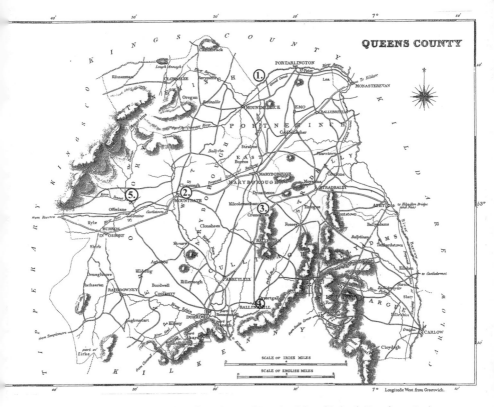

1. Map of Queen's County, taken from Samuel Lewis, *Atlas of Ireland*, (London 1837), showing those places associated with the Trench family mentioned in the text: 1. Garryhinch, 2. Redcastle, 3. Cremorgan, 4. Heywood, 5. Mount Salem.

In 1642 Ballinakill was 'seated among woods in a place so watered with springs as afforded the Earl convenience to make many fish ponds near the Castle he has built there' and 'besides that the town since it had been planted was well inhabited'.[7] In the Cromwellian wars the castle of Ballinakill was taken from the English settlers by the Confederate forces under General Preston with cannon specially sent from Spain. It was soon again besieged from the hills behind by General Fairfax after which the castle was destroyed.[8] The town suffered heavily in these wars, but in 1659 Ballinakill was the third largest town in the county, with a population of 204, one quarter of which was English.[9] Settlers' names from this time included Peet, Browne, Jacob and Stringer.[10]

In 1765 Thomas Ridgeway, earl of Londonderry, died and the town and lands of the manor passed to Philip, Earl Stanhope. Stanhope lived on his estates in England and on the continent and very seldom visited his Irish property, managing the land through agents instead. Ballinakill and its surrounding areas formed a small estate of approximately 1,200 acres and by this time the principal tenant was the Reverend Frederick Trench. In 1770, a few years after his family inherited this Irish property, Lord Stanhope's son, Lord Mahon was living in Geneva in Switzerland,[11] where an extensive memorandum describing every aspect of the Ballinakill property was taken down from a visiting Mr Trench.[12] This was Michael Frederick Trench, always called Frederick, only son of Reverend Trench, who was on close terms with the Stanhope family.[13] This memorandum described the property of 1,100–1,200 acres as being about a mile and a half from north to south and a mile in breadth, and the soil 'most light, excellent for sheep, potatoes and corn'.[14] It goes on to describe every detail of Ballinakill, giving an exact description of the town, its inhabitants and the surrounding area, the local economy and all the businessmen of the town. It then makes many suggestions for the improvement of the place. This long, informative memorandum is one of the first documents in a very extensive correspondence that took place over a period of fifty years between Frederick Trench and Lord Stanhope. It was concerned principally about the property Trench leased from Stanhope, but often gave Stanhope information on many other aspects of his Irish estate. This document was also the first intimation that in 1770 Ballinakill was a town that was on the point of decline, a decline that is then evidenced over the following fifty years in these records.

At the Act of Union in 1800 the marquess of Drogheda, whose pocket borough Ballinakill was by that time, received £15,000 compensation for the loss of the two parliamentary seats, and after this the corporation was allowed to fall into disuse.[15] Ballinakill's loss was compounded by the active development and promotion by the de Vesci's of the town of Abbeyleix, four miles away, and by the development by Lady Ormonde of Castlecomer, a similar distance away. This development attracted firstly the new roads, then Ballinakill's markets and courts, and finally the railway.[16] From then the town went into decline. Up until the development of the modern road system in the nineteenth century, however, Ballinakill was on an important route across the country. It was on the principal road from Dublin to Limerick, and an act of Parliament was obtained for erecting turnpikes at Ballinakill on the road from Athy to Cashel.[17] Both Ballinakill and Trench are marked in Taylor and Skinner's *Maps of the roads of Ireland*, first surveyed in 1777.[18] This lists the road from Dublin to Tipperary going through Ballinakill and where the town is marked, beside the symbol for a gentleman's seat, is the name 'Trench Esq.'[19]

The Trench family traced their ancestry back to a Frederic de la Tranche, a Huguenot refugee who settled in Northumberland in England about 1574 (see figure 2) . His grandson Frederick Trench came to Ireland, settling in Galway in 1631, and it was his son, another Frederick (1633–1704) who married Elizabeth Warburton of Garryhinch in Queen's County.[20] (see figure 1 for Queen's County locations) Her sister, Anna, married his brother John

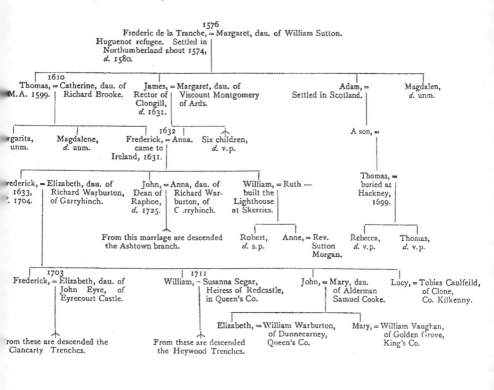

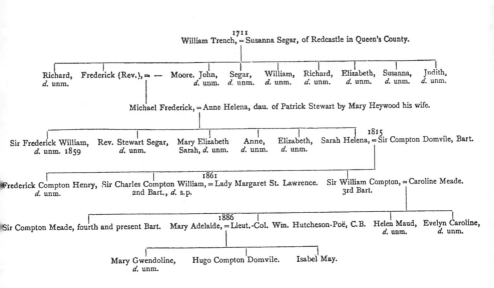

2. Genealogical tables of the Trench family of Heywood.

Trench, dean of Raphoe, and it is from that family that the Ashtown Trenches (with the later title Baron Ashtown) are descended. Frederick and Elizabeth had four children. Their oldest son, Frederick, married Elizabeth Eyre of Eyrecourt Castle in 1703, and this Garbally-based family later became Earls of Clancarty. Their second son, William, came to Queen's County with Charles Coote, later earl of Mountrath, as part of this new wave of developers, doing business in Mountmellick and Mountrath.[21] William married Susanna Segar of Redcastle in Queen's County in 1711 and by 1728 William Trench had leased a house and 157 plantation acres of land in perpetuity from Lord Londonderry at Ballinakill.[22] William and Susanna had nine children. Their second son, Frederick, was born in September 1715[23] and as second son was destined for a career in the church. He went to Trinity College, Dublin where he was ordained in 1740.[24] In 1745 he married Mary Moore,[25] daughter and co-heir of Boyle Moore of Cremorgan, Queen's County. She was a niece of Michael Cox, bishop of Ossory, who was witness to the marriage settlement (where Reverend Trench is described as 'clerk') and she brought Queen's County lands together with £1,200 to the marriage.[26] When his older brother unexpectedly died, Frederick Trench came into properties in Mayo and in Roscommon, making him financially independent, and therefore in a position to live where he chose.[27] Yet he continued to make his home in Ballinakill, where he was a tenant of Lord Londonderry and Lord Stanhope. His house was in the town of Ballinakill itself. The memorandum of 1770 describes 'a house with garden grounds that joins and surrounds the church . . . where he now lives.'[28] Although he still had extensive family links with Queen's County, his son explained the father's action thus:

> Mr William Trench (as assignee to Mr Vigors) was tenant to the Earl of Londonderry; at his decease he was succeeded by his son, the Revd. Frederick Trench, about the year 1742, who finding a large arrear of rent due, actually declined being considered or concerned in the holdings – and so far as being at that day thought an advantageous concern, the then Lord Londonderry relinquished his arrear of £1400 and induced Mr Frederick Trench to become his tenant under the former terms. From 1742–1776 he continued his residence, with considerable improvements, and about that period (having changed his residence to another place) handed over his interests in and near Ballynakill to his only son.[29]

A 1763 traveller described their home thus:

> Near this is a town called Ballynakeil, a very pretty one, where a parson has a sweet habitation. He has 24 acres walled round 10 feet high, the ground naturally in fine slopes and risings, large trees properly dispersed, a river of very clear water running through flowing cascades. These rising grounds command very extensive views.[30]

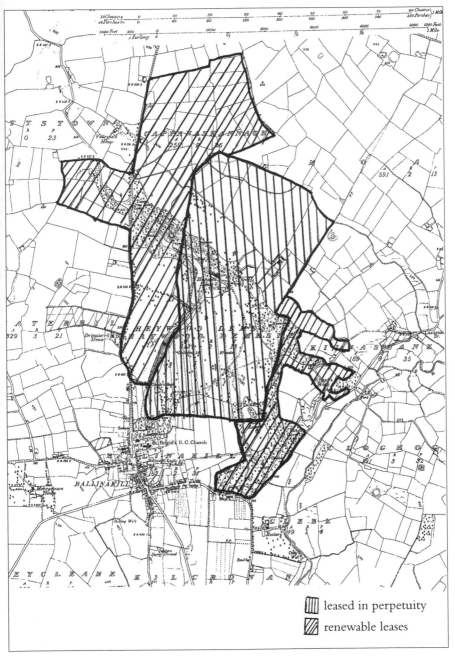

3. Showing those areas leased by Frederick Trench, and the townland 'Heywood Demesne'. Based on the first Ordnance Survey map of 1838.

That Reverend Trench had begun to improve his property is also referred to in the 1770 memorandum where it mentions 'some springs that are intended to be turned to form some water in Mr Trench's improvements, and which afterwards may be of considerable utility to the town'.[31] These improvements are described as work which 'may render it inferior to few country residences in Ireland'.[32]

By 1770 his father had taken a total of 258 acres beside the village in a number of leases from Lord Stanhope.[33] The principal lease was one for the house and demesne with 180 acres which in 1770 was at a rent of 12 shillings an acre. By then Reverend Trench also held a further 52 acres in perpetuity, 14 acres for twenty-one years, and 12 acres for nine years, making a total area of 258 acres[34] (see figure 3). In the Stanhope Irish estate rentals from 1767 on, the agent, Mr Delaney, lists Reverend Trench as having the 'tenement and land backyards and garden' at £131.3s.0d.[35] This entry continued yearly. In 1773 he had moved to the top of the tenants' list and was paying a yearly rent of £145.13s.0d. for a tenement and land in Ballinakill, with backyard and garden.[36]

Frederick and Susanna's only son, Michael Frederick, was born in May 1746. He was educated in Kilkenny College[37] and in Trinity College Dublin where he graduated in 1766. He went on to study in London, in the Middle Temple, and was called to the Irish Bar in 1774.[38] In 1774 he married Anne-Helena Stewart, only daughter and heiress of Patrick Stewart and his wife Mary Heywood.[39] Reverend Trench decided to settle his Connacht estates on his son and a thousand pounds a year on him and his wife.[40] He arranged with Lord Stanhope to make the Ballinakill leases over to his son[41] and wrote to Frederick 'You shall have the sole direction and management of the lands to alter and improve them and so as best suits your fancy'.[42]

Frederick Trench began this alteration and improvement almost imme-diately. In 1775, in looking for a further 32 acres, he wrote to Lord Stanhope:

> 'Twould be our wish and purpose to build in the adjacent demesne. . . . The improvements intended are considerable, and must be expensive. Tis probable in the course of the next six years there will be in building, walling, and plantations an expenditure of £5,000 in your Lordship's town and among your tenantry.[43]

He continued:

> for if I do not find your Lordship's kindness to coincide with my wishes, I must look for a settlement in another quarter of Ireland; and quit the spot I am the most attached to on earth, and the neighbourhood I should most prefer to live in . . . we would willingly give a guinea per acre for the pasturable ground and half a guinea for that which will be under wood and water.

£5,000 was indeed a large amount of money, five times the annual sum his father had settled on him.

In 1775, Frederick Trench and his newly-wed wife visited Lord Stanhope in England. There he showed Stanhope the design for a new house he planned to build and, as security for this investment in the property, tried to negotiate a long lease for the balance of the property, while the core acres were held in perpetuity under the older lease. Lord Stanhope would agree to a twenty-one year lease only, renewable every seven years, but he cautioned Mr Trench 'to consider how he made such a family establishment as he, Lord Stanhope, could not be answerable for those who might come after him'.[44] To copperfasten this agreement, Trench had a transcript of the meeting considered by legal council, and then it was sent to Lord Stanhope's agent to put in hand when the leases would come up for renewal. Based on this assurance, Frederick Trench was able to proceed with work on his plans for the estate. His intention was first to build his new house which may have been designed by his friend from his days in London, the architect James Gandon[45] and then to start the considerable task of remodelling the Ballinakill landscape into his romantic vision. As a much older man he was to write in 1827:

> A most beautiful romantic site . . . My attachment to it has nearly been fatal to me the sum expended in buildings and ornamental improvements has been upward of £45,000. I state it without vanity or boasting, but with sincere regret instead of removing to some of those neighbouring properties of which we possessed the fee I unguardedly continued to expand here.[46]

Most of the correspondence between Frederick Trench and Lord Stanhope concerns the land and Trench's attempts to buy it out, with many details of the various leases by which it was held. He made several efforts, particularly as a young man in 1775, and then as an old man in 1827, when he wrote to Lord Stanhope:

> I believe it is more than half a century since I wrote to that most respectable old nobleman your grandfather, who then resided at Geneva, relative to my wish to be considered as a willing purchaser, should the property come to be disposed as was then reported (but in error).

He continued 'My wish would be to be permitted to become a purchaser of the arrondisment of my demesne at a fair and just valuation by a competent person; I should not look for any possible or personal advantage'.[47]

These negotiations and attempts to arrive at an agreed price are carefully detailed in the correspondence. In 1827 Trench wrote to Stanhope that, while eighteen years was then the usual rate of purchase for leases in perpetuity, 'I would willingly give twenty years' purchase for the whole, which I hope may extract your Lordship's approbation'.[48] His son Frederick, a professional soldier and once a regular visitor to Chevening, the Stanhope seat in Kent, had also written to Stanhope urging the purchase, only to receive the response

I have no recollection whatever of my having made to you now after my father's death or at any other time the promise which you suppose of selling to your father such portions of my Irish estate as he might wish, nor could I be reasonably expected to do so.[49]

Stanhope's position was that he was willing to sell the whole Irish estate, but only as a complete unit, and he was not willing to sell separately the Heywood demesne and those other Ballinakill properties to Trench. Two years after Frederick had died, and after lengthy correspondence about the purchase, Stanhope wrote a final letter to young Frederick who had now inherited the property:

Your proposal of giving 20 years purchase for the Perpetuities is the same which Mr Freshfield [his banker] considered to be inadmissible and I believe that I communicated to you above two years ago the letter which he wrote to me upon the subject . . . that at that price I could not reinvest the purchase money without loss. This is the plain and simple view I take of the question and I am therefore obliged to decline your offer.[50]

While Trench's efforts to buy in the 1820s came to nothing, it is ironic that, following the appearance of potato blight and the tragic series of famines in Ireland in the 1840s, Lord Stanhope was scratching around in order to find someone, anyone to buy his Irish estates. In 1846 he asked Thomas Vesey to approach Lord de Vesci of the neighbouring estate of Abbeyleix, offering de Vesci the purchase of the Ballinakill estate 'of which I am least disinclined to part' describing it as 1,444 acres with a rent of £2018.1s.9d.[51] In 1847 he wrote waspishly to his son, Lord Mahon, that he had offered it to Sir Compton Domvile, but he 'returned no answer and I believe that Sir F. Trench is in such a pecuniary situation that, so far from being able to acquire an estate which is worth £50,000, he could not afford to pay £500.'[52] In 1848 in mounting panic he wrote to Freshfield

It appears to me that the chief obstacle to Sales of Property in Ireland arises from the disturbed and dangerous condition of that country, and the Ballynakill Estate becomes much less profitable than it was, partly from the reductions which it is requisite to make in the Rents, and partly from defalcations in their payment.[53]

His panic was justified. Ballinakill estate was not sold. Mary Trench lived on in Heywood, managing the estate very effectively with her brother Frederick. When they died their leases passed to the Domvile family through the marriage of their sister to Sir Compton Domvile of Templeogue and Santry, in Dublin. In the end the Stanhope estates in Queen's County were purchased by the Irish Land Commission under the 1885 Land Purchase (Ireland) Act for £26,674 for eighty-eight holdings.[54] The demesne of Heywood was bought

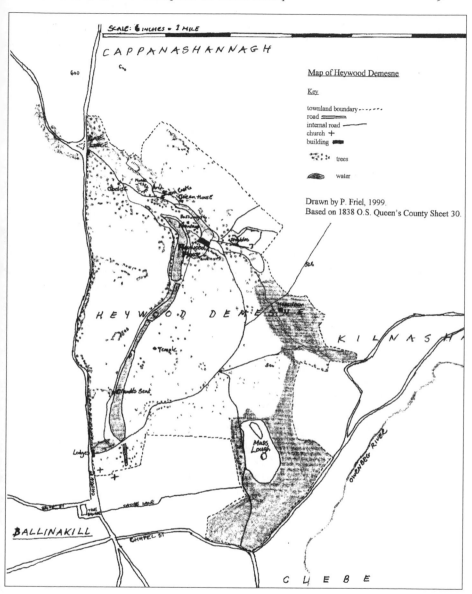

4. Map of Heywood Demesne.

in 1895 by Sir William Hutcheson Poe, who had married Adelaide Domvile, and these lands were finally bought out for £2,785 and distributed among the tenants by the Irish Land Commission under the 1923 Land Act.[55]

Frederick Trench – his interests and influences

Michael Frederick Trench (always called Frederick) was born in May 1746. In 1753, when he was six years old, he began his education in Kilkenny College twenty miles from home.[1] This long established school was then under the patronage of Michael Cox, the bishop of Ossory, his mother's uncle. His father, Reverend Trench, held his position in this diocese, as did his mother's sister's husband, Reverend Hugh Dawson. Ten pupils enrolled in Kilkenny College during 1753, ranging in age from six to sixteen. Frederick was the youngest pupil. When his initial education was completed, Frederick went on to study in Trinity College, Dublin, as had his father before him, and he graduated as a Batchelor of Arts in 1766.[2] Then a young man in his early twenties, he went to London to study law in Middle Temple. In 1770, aged twenty-four, he borrowed several sums of money: £1,000 with his address given at Middle Temple and a further £1,000 and £400, both to his Ballinakill address.[3] These monies presumably were needed to support his student years in London. His studies successfully completed, he was called to the Irish Bar in 1774.[4]

It was during these years in London that Frederick Trench joined a group that would be central to his adult life. Largely from Ireland, this group of young connoisseurs represented particular aspects of the Enlightenment in that their membership was determined not strictly by class but by their education (often Grand-tour influenced), uniting them in their interests in contemporary art, architecture and science, which they then returned to put into effect in Ireland, initially in Dublin and subsequently throughout their various estates in Ireland. This group found one particular focus in a Sunday evening salon which had developed in the house of the English artist, Paul Sandby, and these evenings are described by one important member of that group, the architect James Gandon, as ones where 'friends assembled and formed a conversazione on the arts, the sciences, and the general literature of the day.'[5] The Sandbys themselves are interesting. There were two brothers, Paul and Thomas, both of whom were founder members of the Royal Academy. Paul (1731–1809) had trained as a military draughtsman with the Ordnance Survey of Scotland[6] and was an accomplished printmaker and landscape artist. His brother Thomas (1723–98) was deputy ranger of Windsor Great Park where he carried out considerable landscape work for the duke of Cumberland, younger brother of King George II. Thomas was also the first professor of architecture in the Royal Academy. Together the Sandbys played an active role in publicising and exhibiting art, and 'effected a profound change in the status of artists and their relationship with the public'.[7] In later life Frederick Trench would be a regular attendee at the Academy Exhibitions, commenting on the works on view there.[8] In the course of his travels around England he visited many properties and described any current building works he saw. He also visited many exhibitions and other contemporary artistic events, such as Lord Elgin's house where he saw 'there exhibits every Saturday and Tuesday at noon in a covered Area, almost all the Frieze of the Parthenon, or Temple of Minerva at Athens, and a quantity of broken stuff – which he wants the Parliament to purchase at £20.00 – Bravo!'[9]

In the Sandby salon Frederick Trench joined with his friends and contemporaries. These were mostly influential connoisseurs such as John Dawson, Lord Carlow and later earl of Portarlington who was also from Queen's County.[10] Another friend was the earl of Charlemont, collector and builder of the wonderful Casino at Marino outside Dublin. Another was the architect James Gandon. Yet another was Sackville Hamilton who was to become permanent undersecretary in the chief secretary's office. Sackville's brother, Captain Hamilton, was another member of the Sandby salon, as were Lord Duncannon, Mr Wyndham, Sir Richard Musgrave and Trench's lifelong friend Andrew Caldwell. There they would discuss art, architecture and the latest literature as well as their plans for their own properties.[11] It is certain that they also discussed current affairs and potential developments in Dublin in particular because, on returning to Dublin, Frederick Trench joined several others of this group in becoming a member of the Dublin Wide Streets Commission. Established by statute in 1757 to open up Dublin's Parliament Street, these Wide Streets Commissioners were empowered to develop the city of Dublin, to plan, to buy land and to lease it to speculators to develop to agreed designs. In 1779 the group was instrumental in persuading the architect James Gandon to come to Dublin to work on these developments and design the new Custom House for the developing city. This second half of the eighteenth century was a time of great energy and confidence in Dublin, and as a member of this powerful group Trench attended the Commissioners' meetings very regularly in the period 1780–1800.[12]

While still a law student the young Frederick Trench took advantage of a lull in that century's struggles between Britain and France to travel to Europe in the years between 1770 and 1772 on what is now called the Grand Tour. This 'moving academy' was particularly fashionable among educated upper- and middle-class people and, as they enthusiastically experienced the differing climates, dramatic scenery and antique ruins in those countries through which they travelled, the Tour was of particular interest to those interested in art and classicism. Travelling via Paris, Trench several times visited Lord Stanhope, his landlord, who lived in Geneva.[13] He called on him first in 1770 and again with his wife in 1775.[14] At this time Geneva, a French-speaking Protestant area, was growing in importance as a stop on the Tour for many British visitors.[15] Its dramatic mountainous landscapes particularly appealed to those with an interest in scenery. Trench was later to name one area of his Ballinakill lands 'Lucerne' and another area, a lake he created, 'Lac Omon', after memorable sights in Switzerland. Incidentally, to fall ill was a great hazard for a traveller in a foreign country. In France in 1770 Frederick consulted a Doctor Tissot, who diagnosed a 'too great motion of the nervous system' and prescribed absolute quiet and a measured life. He also recommended a diet of vegetables, no tea, coffee, wine or chocolate, not too much milk and no eggs. The patient was not to sit up late, but to rise early, ride frequently and to take warm baths.[16]

During the same period, in 1772 and 1774, Trench was in correspondence with the painter David Allen. Allen, a Scot, was a very accomplished painter who spent the years 1767–77 in Italy, where he studied and worked. He also assisted such travellers as Trench in acquiring works of art.[17] In 1772 David Allen wrote to Trench (c/o St James' Coffeehouse, London) describing in detail the subjects and the progress of those paintings Trench had ordered from him. Describing many to Trench as 'most picturesque', and in proposing classical subjects Allan wrote 'You very possibly remember them'. He also suggested Trench study prints of these subjects 'by which means you will have some idea of their beautys'.[18] We have no firm evidence that Trench did in fact visit Allen in Rome. But in 1774 Allan listed the completed collection he was now arranging to ship back to Ireland. He described a 'whole collection arranged', the choice of 'subjects ancient, they being also elegant, expressive and sublime, I heartily wish for the propagation of good taste and the good of art. I wish that more people were in that good way of thinking'.[19] The 1772 letter also writes 'Hewston offers you his best respects'.[20] This was Christopher Hewetson (1737–98), from Thomastown, County Kilkenny, who worked as a sculptor in Rome from 1765 until 1798.[21] Hewetson was also on commission from Trench to sell some prints on his behalf. Whether these prints were by Trench himself or another is not clear. In the 1774 letter, sent via Mrs Pole, Trench's neighbour at Ballyfin, Allan looked for a payment of 288 Italian sequins for this collection, an amount equalling about £144.[22] This cost may be compared to the rent of £180 Trench was paying for his Queen's County lands at this time. That he incurred much debt at this period is confirmed by his father's letter where he stated that 'I think £7,000 will pay off all debts whatsoever'.[23] His wife's marriage settlement of £8,000[24] must have been used to pay these debts as we know from a letter to her children 'From the improvident use your father made secretly of some of my money to pay extravagant debts incurred early in life mostly abroad you are all sufferers'.[25] She clearly did not share her husband's enthusiasm for these purchases.

Frederick Trench returned to Ireland in 1774. He was called to the Irish Bar and in the same year married Anne Helena Stewart, a cousin of his great friend Andrew Caldwell, who was a named party in their marriage settlement.[26] His wife was the only daughter and heiress of Patrick Stewart and his wife Mary Heywood of Drogheda. She was also a cousin of the Stewarts of Killymoon Castle, County Tyrone. Trench's neighbour, Mrs Pole, wrote 'We rejoice to think that you have every prospect of Rational Happiness' with 'one, that from your description, I shall think very Amiable'.[27] To mark this union a series of lovely oval pastels was commissioned from the accomplished and fashionable Irish portrait painter Hugh Douglas Hamilton. Now in the National Gallery of Ireland, these portraits are of the newlyweds Frederick and Anne (figure 5), of her mother Mrs Heywood, and of his parents, Reverend and Mrs Trench.[28] This may be a posthumous portrait of Mrs Trench, because, although the date of her death is unknown, Reverend Trench was a widower in January 1775.[29] There is a lovely contrast between the plain, rather solid appearance of the Trench parents, he in his cleric's robes, and she in black and white, and that of Mrs Stewart with her intelligent face, elegant bones, her stylish hair and ermine collaret. Young Frederick, 'never better than when in a bustle and hurry',[30] has an enthusiastic appearance, with stylishly powdered hair, fine cravat and cuffs. His new wife is very fashionably dressed with a large pearl necklace and earrings.

After Anne Stewart and Frederick Trench married, according to custom her mother lived with them, and it is her maiden name, Heywood, they gave to the lands in Ballinakill. An inscription on the mausoleum built in the grounds reads: 'Sacred to the memory of Mary Heywood (by marriage Stewart). Her

5. Frederick Trench and his wife Anne Helena Stewart

posterity revere her virtues, these grounds not undeservedly retain her name. If worth, benevolence, religion and gentleness of manners avail, she doth not sleep forever.' Reverend Trench arranged with Lord Stanhope to make the leases over to his son, and wrote to Frederick 'You shall have the sole direction and management of the lands to alter and improve them and so as best sates your fancy'.[31] As was customary, Reverend Trench planned to vacate the property to his son and new wife. By now Reverend Trench was a widower and although the marriage settlement covered the possibility of his remarrying, he wrote that his

> winter quarters for the future must be Dublin, Birr or wherever else providence may direct. Mt Salem[32] is too retired a spot for a single person at my time of life to venture to pass away the melancholy winter hours all alone without help, without a friend, where the noise of waters and the storms among dismantled trees can only save to remind him that his end is approaching![33]

We do not know whether he retired or not but it seems he did move to Mount Salem, where he had almost 400 acres. This estate passed in turn to Frederick's second son in 1815, the clergyman Reverend Stewart Segar Trench.[34] In 1770, Frederick had unsuccessfully tried to get the living of Ballinakill from Lord Stanhope for his father,[35] a position that the grandson was to later hold. In 1775 Reverend Trench was installed as chancellor of Emly and rector of Templeichally in the diocese of Cashel. This he held until his death in 1790. He, too, is buried at the mausoleum in Heywood.

Now that his education and travels were complete and he was successfully married, Frederick Trench lost no time in beginning what was to be his life's work, a very ambitious and extensive plan to establish, improve and romanticise the 250-acre estate now to be known as 'Heywood'. This entire undertaking was based on his particular eighteenth-century understanding of what constituted the ideal landscape. In the previous century, a garden had been an enclosed area of very formal construction, surrounded by a wall. This garden was a protected 'civilised' area, maintained very deliberately against wild and rampant nature outside. In 1763 Reverend Trench lived in the town of Ballinakill in a house with '24 acres of pleasure gardens walled around ten feet high.'[36] In Ireland of course these walls could also serve as defensive measures, or at least to keep the natives outside this boundary that separated the new civilisation from uncomprehending native wildness.

As the eighteenth century progressed, as their wealth and security increased, people began to look out beyond their protected enclosures and, with growing confidence, to expand their gardens and pleasure grounds outwards. But this expansion was carried out within a clearly understood set of precepts. These precepts were first described in the writings of Alexander Pope, then depicted in the landscapes of Claude and Poussin and their many followers, and enhanced by the experiences of the 'academy'[37] of the Grand Tour. Thus the notion of the picturesque, of what was 'beautiful', gradually emerged as a way of looking at nature informed by the hindsight of art: Claude, Poussin and Salvator Rosa provided a new framework for the appreciation of landscape.[38] The simple contemplation of landscape came to be regarded as an important pursuit for cultivated people and almost in itself the practice of an art. To express a correct taste in landscape was a valuable social accomplishment, as valuable as being able to sing well, or to compose a polite letter.[39] The idea of nature as something to be tamed and controlled was paramount and to create such an arcadian landscape it was necessary to impose a vision of perfection, a better, civilised form and understanding on that landscape's native state. As government control became established in Ireland the country became peaceful. As the prices for agricultural produce rose, the leisured interest and the financial resources for the development of these gardens and pleasuregrounds began to spread through the country. In an area such as Queen's County, which was particularly good grazing land, the third generation of plantation families like Trench had taste, leisure and wealth enough to indulge these romantic landscape interests.

I have subtitled this book *The creation of a Romantic landscape* so it may be helpful at this point to explain in detail what is meant by a romantic landscape and how romantic landscaping was a physical manifestation and extension of what is known as the Romantic Movement. With its emphasis on emotion over reason, the initial inspiration for this movement came from the Frenchman Jean Jacques Rousseau who said 'I felt before I thought'. Coming from 'romancelike', or the strange and fanciful nature of mediaeval romances, the Romantic Movement was characterised by a reliance on the imagination, a subjectivity of approach, freedom of thought and expression and an idealisation of nature. Thus imagination was praised over reason, emotion over logic, and intuition over science. The illusion of immediate experience was all-important. This theory was applied to landscape. A carefully arranged series of scenes and vistas was intended to present the viewer with a range of experiences and emotions. A distant hill with a ruin suggested an earlier, simpler time. A cliff, a waterfall or a cave hinted at the awful power of nature. A mausoleum inspired melancholy thoughts of loss and tragedy.

To arrange a romantic landscape correctly, Pope's fundamental principle for laying out a garden and then siting buildings and structures within it had to be adhered to. This was based on the importance of first discovering the 'genius loci' or the spirit or presence of the place. Once this was identified, then, almost as if painting a picture, the scene could be improved by planting and by placing appropriate decorative buildings in it.[40] From a position, often on a height, the discerning eye would then be drawn into the distance by a series of objects, in a 'complex of associations and meanings, in which each object bore a specific and analysable relationship to the others'.[41] This was the principal that informed the layout of Heywood. As Frederick Trench created his ideal landscape, over the next twenty-five years he fashioned an entire romantic world, damning rivers, creating lakes, remodelling the landscape and elaborating and accenting that landscape with a series of exquisite buildings or follies, in his own words elaborating and accenting 'so perfectly what it ought to be that you would imagine nature (and not a whirligig) had been the Creative Power.'[42] He inscribed a quotation from Pope, which exemplified his work:

> To smooth the lawn, to decorate the dale,
> To swell the summit, or to scoop the vale,
> To mark each distance through each opening glade,
> Mass kindred tints or vary shade from shade,
> To bend the arch, to ornament the grot,
> In all – let nature never be forgot.
> Her varied gifts with sparing hand combine,
> Paint as you plant and as you work design.[43]

A letter from the recently wed Trench to Lord Stanhope in 1775 explained how he wanted to build a new house in the adjacent demesne and planned to spend £5,000 in the next six years in 'building, walling and plantations'.[44] In November 1776 he wrote he 'should be very happy to have it in my power to acquaint my Lord what considerable improvements I have been at all this summer'.[45] In December 1814 'it was very late and actually dark when I came in . . . from attending the entire day to the workmen'.[46]

Trench began by building this new house on a height looking out on the soft hills and valleys, which descend to the town of Ballinakill, although the town was not visible from the house. It has been suggested that this house was designed by James Gandon but this is rejected by McParland in his definitive study.[47] Although clearly influenced by Gandon, it is much more likely to have been designed by the amateur architect, Trench himself 'after his own plan' as his contemporary Sir Charles Coote states in 1801.[48] A drawing by James Malton shows the entrance front of a simple three-bay house, two stories high, with the date 1789 inscribed over the entrance door (figure 6). This is one of Malton's first exhibited works, shown in the Society of Artists in London in 1790.[49] Coote states that 'the apartments are as commodious as could be wished for, and are considerably more extensive, than we should suppose from the outside view'.[50] The house in Heywood was subsequently very thoroughly remodelled and extended, most extensively by its new owner Lieutenant-Colonel William Hutcheson-Poe after 1898 when Trench's original building

6. The original house at Heywood by James Malton, 1790

was absorbed into the centre of these subsequent building works. This remodelled house was accidentally burned down in 1950 by which time it was owned by the Salesian order. It was tumbled in on its cellars and grassed over, and this grassed mound is now its only visible remains. However the site is clearly outlined by the twentieth-century Lutyens-designed gardens which later surrounded it.

To return to the mid-eighteenth century from 1774 onwards Frederick Trench divided his time between Ballinakill and Dublin. In Dublin he spent the winter season in his house in Palace Row on the northern side of fashionable Rutland (now Parnell) Square, facing the Rotunda Gardens. Palace Row was a new street formed in 1769 as a continuation of Gardiner's Row along the north side of the Rotunda Gardens. In 1786 his Wide Streets Commissioners spent £1,100 in beautifying the gardens, now renamed Rutland Square.[51] This area of Dublin was highly fashionable. His neighbours included many society figures, members of parliament, and friends such as Andrew Caldwell and of course Lord Charlemont in his wonderful town house on the same side of the square.[52]

Trench travelled frequently to Dublin, where he was a cultured man about town. He attended art auctions,[53] and was a very regular presence at the meetings of the Wide Streets Commissioners. From 1785–90 he was the member for Maryborough in the Irish House of Commons,[54] where his first interest was to promote the development of the grounds of Rutland Square, opposite his own house. In 1785 he presented a bill 'For the more effectual lighting and watching Rutland Square, and for the better support and maintenance of the Lying-in Hospital, and for other purposes therein mentioned'.[55] He also promoted his interest in the Wide Streets Commissioners by proposing two bills to advance their work. In 1787 he put forward a 'Bill for the further explaining and amending the several acts now in force for making wide and convenient passages in the city of Dublin'.[56] In 1790 he introduced 'An Act for the improvement of the City of Dublin by making wide and convenient passages through the same and for regulating the coal trade.'[57] In 1786 he proposed a vote of £2,500 for the 'Dublin Society for improving husbandry and other useful Arts',[58] and he became a member of that society himself in 1792.[59]

By now Trench was publicly acknowledged to be a reputable amateur architect – architecture only very recently having evolved as a profession – with a keen interest in all related matters. In 1784 the Board of Dublin's Rotunda Hospital decided to increase the rooms available for public entertainment at the Hospital. The Rotunda Assembly Rooms were used for social functions, including indoor promenades – a wet-weather alternative to the promenade in the Rotunda Gardens.[60] These earned considerable sums of money for the hospital funds. In 1784 a set of drawings and proposals for the new rooms was submitted to the board. And in a meeting on 8 June 1784 it was ordered that the plans submitted by Frederick Trench, amateur architect, who was elected a governor of the hospital on the same day, be sent to James Gandon for his opinion.[61] Trench's plans survive in the hospital records. While the building is attributed to the architect Richard Johnston, the original idea and plans were Trench's and as a member of the building committee he remained actively involved in its execution. The building committee consisted of the duke of Leinster, Lord Charlemont, Luke Gardiner, David La Touche, William Bury, Dr. Rock and Frederick Trench.[62] Frederick Trench supervised many details of this building including the Coade stone external decoration, which he also used in Heywood.[63] In 1786 Trench was authorised to choose the ornaments to be used in 'the Elevation of the new Buildings to Cavendish-street, as he may judge proper and conducive to the advantages of this Charity'.[64] Here he included the arms of his friend the duke of Rutland, lord-lieutenant of Ireland, in this pediment, together with the star of the new Order of St. Patrick. The *Dublin Freeman's Journal* wrote of these new Assembly Rooms as being 'superb beyond description'.[65]

In discussing the Rotunda, Gandon described Trench as 'a gentleman of large fortune, and great taste in the Fine Arts, who devoted his time and his unwearied exertions, to promote by every means in his power the improvement of every department of this noble charitable institution'.[66] He went on to suggest that in gratitude a statue to Trench's memory should be raised in the hospital. This was never done. During the January-to-April season these buildings were used for concerts, cards and balls which were very popular and highly successful.[67] But the political unrest in the following years meant that promenades had to be abandoned and the new rooms used as a barracks. The Act of Union in 1801 and the subsequent removal of the parliament resulted in the decline of the fashionable high society that supported these rooms. They survive substantially unchanged however, and now house the Ambassador cinema and the Gate Theatre.

In 1782 a committee was set up to consider how the proposed extension to the House of Lords should be 'best constructed in order to unite with the General Plan of Improvement of the City now under consideration'.[68] This committee was chaired by Lord Carlow, with the duke of Leinster, the earl of Tyrone and the earl of Charlemont, and assisted by Frederick Trench and Sackville Hamilton. The committee settled on a plan by James Gandon. In 1787, the House of Commons was also considering expansion with a new entrance to the west on land to be acquired from the Wide Streets Commissioners. A Commons committee was appointed with Samuel Hayes of Avondale and Frederick Trench its principal members.[69] While a design of James Gandon was also adopted here, the work was executed by another architect, Robert Parke.

After the Act of Union in 1801, however, the Houses of Commons and of Lords became redundant. Instead of proceeding with a plan to acquire land between Westmoreland Street and the river to build a new headquarters, the Bank of Ireland acquired the House of Lords for its new offices. When the bank was established in 1783, Frederick Trench had been one of the original subscribers to the capital of the Bank of Ireland, with a deposit of £2,000. The board of the bank set up a building committee in 1802 to oversee a competition for this conversion, with Andrew Caldwell, Frederick Trench and Sackville Hamilton as adjudicators.[70] These three did not agree however, and published their differing views in *Thoughts on the Appropriation of the Parliament House for the National Bank*.[71] During this remodelling, in 1804, Trench acquired ten capitals from columns in the late parliament house. He wrote at the time '[I] hope should any chance conduct any of the Board in the line of my residence they will allow me the pleasure of showing them how these will be applied to use'.[72] It is not known where Trench might have thought to use them in Heywood, but in 1906 Edwin Lutyens incorporated four elaborate capitals in the outer side of his garden building there.

In 1794 Trench was appointed a governor of Doctor Steeven's Hospital.[73] At the same time, he continued his other interests with the Wide Streets Commissioners. In 1785, houses in Dame Street were ordered to be embellished with 'such additional stone work as may be necessary according to Mr

Trench's Designs.'[74] Many of the Commissioners were actively involved in development and Trench owned ten building lots on North Frederick Street. He was allowed to design these as he wished.

Trench's work and written views on art and architecture are clear. He was a thoroughly conventional, pro-establishment representative of his class. Neither he nor his immediate circle had any interest in the Irish political movements of his time. As a member of the House of Commons he must have been aware of the efforts of his contemporaries, but his real and almost only passion was for reading and building in Heywood. At the same time the political events culminating in the 1798 rebellion must have exercised all his family and contemporaries. Indeed the area lying between Ballinakill and Castlecomer – only a few miles from Heywood – was where the United Irishmen Miles Byrne and Fr John Murphy together with the colliers of the Castlecomer hills fought against General Asgill. Three croppies were subsequently executed in Ballinakill itself in 1798.[75] In the Rotunda records there is a memorial which Trench sent to Lord Cornwallis in 1798. In this he described how by building walls and gates, he had prevented between 700 and 1,000 men from meeting or travelling by road in from Drumcondra. He then requested some payment for this.[76]

Trench described the local situation in a later letter to Lord Stanhope when he included a drawing of how the markethouse had been made 'almost a citadel', and described the tenants of Ballinakill as 'the best chance of a defensive security of any I know'. He went on to say that, as County Kildare between Ballinakill and Dublin was 'known to take the lead', his ladies had returned to Dublin and 'lost the comforts of a charming autumn in a beautiful place'.[77] This does not give the impression of someone actively concerned about the political scene, if the principal drawback of the unsettled situation was to miss the autumn leaves.

After the Act of Union, however, the Ireland Frederick Trench knew changed for ever. The society he knew and enjoyed altered drastically and Dublin – no longer the seat of parliament – never recovered the vitality it once had. In 1819, feeling his seventy-three years he wrote:

> The Union and the changes have made most desperate progress among my contemporaries. I now cannot attempt forming intercourse with the rising generation, to them it would be dull, to me wearisome and from the most refined and civilised district in the Kingdom, not one person remains of the age in which I lived.[78]

He and his family had always travelled over and back to England, often spending several months at a time there. They visited many fashionable places – Bath, Southampton, Cheltenham, Winchester (where his son Frederick was stationed with the army) – and spent long periods in Birmingham and

7. View of the Entrance Gate from Dublin to Heywood Queen's Co.
The Seat of Frederick Trench Esquire.

London. They often met their extended family, 'of immediate cousins we have not less than thirty';[79] 'we are quite surrounded by cousins by one side or another'[80] and 'meet many old friends: the Colonel and Mrs Heywood and all nephews, nieces, or their families'.[81] They visited the 'Ladies of Llangollen' regularly en route across Wales 'and were much amused, their library seems valuable and well chosen.'[82]

For all he enjoyed travelling, as he got older the pleasures of London began to pall. He became more melancholic, as he wrote in 1806 'I declare I quit it now without regret – forever I think. I walk much slower, I recollect scenes forty years past, and friends thirty years dead'.[83] As he got older, Heywood gave him more and more pleasure.

> I cannot conceive (on a small scale) a more perfect scene than from whence I now sit. Some nature, much art, (the pursuit of a long life, which when urging to a close I am over apt to think might have been applied to better purpose) have produced an effect it would be a real gratification to submit to those we regard.[84]

They had many visitors. 'I am rather inclined to call our life here that of seclusion, than retirement. We have little or no intercourse with the country,

8. View from the Dublin Approach to Heywood in the Queens County Ireland.
The Seat of Frederick Trench Esquire.

but are seldom without some friends and often are full stored.'[85] These friends
came to talk and to admire his creation at Heywood.

In the intervening years, Frederick Trench had done enormous work at
Heywood. He demolished hills, mounded up other hills, made roads, and then
improved this landscape with gatehouses, obelisks, ruins, temples, viewpoints,
eyecatchers, an orangerie, a bathhouse, a summerhouse and a grotto. He built
a mortuary for his mother-in-law, his wife and then for his own remains when
his life would end. His house was on a height overlooking his idyllic landscape
with the ground falling away to his lakes below. The Kilkenny artist, John
Comerford (c.1770–1832)[86] drew two miniature portraits of the elderly
Frederick Trench and of his wife, Anne. This elderly Trench is portrayed as an
open-faced man who, from his ruddy complexion, could easily be imagined
as having spent much time outdoors.

In 1818 his son, Frederick William Trench, made a series of views of
Heywood which were engraved and printed for circulation. Six of these are
known. As his father was still very active at this time it is certain that he was
closely interested in these. Young Frederick was a keen draftsman and many
other drawings of his survive, as well as some drawings of his fathers. In this
set of etchings, the romantic landscape of Heywood is set out in all its
splendour, from the approach through the entrance gate with the house in the

distance (figure 7). The scenery reveals itself as the traveller draws nearer to the house (figures 8 and 9). Then there are the views which are seen from the house itself looking out from the windows of the 'drawing room at Heywood' (figures 10 and 11). As these were done during Frederick Trench's lifetime and by his son, they are likely to be correct in all details. They lay out this world for the viewer much more clearly than any written description could.

So we can imagine these two men, father and son, sitting in the drawing room of their house, a room described by Trench as one where 'the comforts of blending a library and drawing in one is very great, and access to books (where uncompelled) really an indulgence.'[87] From the gable window they looked out on a lake, with orangerie, gothic ruins and windows, sham castle, and entrance gates placed throughout the little hills. The other window looked southward in the direction of the (unseen) village, over further lakes, with bridges, a classic seat named 'Mount Salem Seat' in the first Ordnance Survey map of 1838, (later called 'Claude's Seat') and the Temple of the Winds placed overlooking all on a distant hill.

The whole was a wonder of taste and perfection.

> Nature has been so truly copied, that in none of the most numberous elegant improvements is seen anything of artificial appearance. The most delightful scenes are presented to the eye, and the senses of some voluptuaries would indeed be ravished with views of such exquisite beauty.[88]

Frederick Trench in Ballinakill

Although they owned considerable land in Queen's County, in Mayo and in Roscommon, it is clear that the Trench family continued to make their home in Ballinakill. But as long as the owner of those lands, Lord Stanhope, refused to let them buy out their leases, then regardless of how secure their tenancy was, they would always remain just tenants in Queen's County. Even though an 1801 list of the resident gentry of the barony named Frederick Trench, Esq. of Heywood,[1] Trench was not, in fact, the landowner.

This would certainly have coloured his standing among his peers in that community because, for example, not actually owning the land, he was therefore ineligible to become a member of the grand jury. This was the primary organ of local government, a local administration with responsibility for roads, bridges, gaols, infirmaries and which was selected from the leading property owners in each county.[2] The single documented time Frederick Trench was active at this county level was in 1777 as a young man back developing his home in Ballinakill. He was then appointed county sheriff, 'that disagreeable office'.[3] Appointed by the lord lieutenant, this post had no specific property qualifications but holders were expected to be resident in the county.[4] As the post carried a substantial financial burden considerable personal wealth was needed and this may well be one factor in Frederick Trench's appointment to the post, and also perhaps why he did not pursue this aspect of public life.[5] Thus, apart from the years 1785 to 1790 when Trench was member for Maryborough in the Irish House of Commons,[6] he took little part in local politics. Even as an M.P. he promoted his own architectural interests and those of the Dublin Wide Streets Commissioners rather than any local Queen's County issues.

In 1800 the gentlemen of the Queen's County met to discuss a proposal to build a canal from Monasterevan to Castlecomer to link the collieries there to the Grand Canal. This canal was to run via Ballinakill, and while the accompanying map shows Heywood, Frederick Trench's name is nowhere to be seen, neither as one of the committee nor as a subscriber to the scheme.[7] This confirms that Trench was not counted among the land-owning gentlemen of the county. Whether or not his financial support for the scheme was sought is not known, possibly because, unlike the landowners, he would have had no vested interest in such a scheme either as a potential investor or beneficiary. His later attempts to buy out the Heywood land may have been motivated to a lesser degree by this tenant position. For all these reasons it seems that he had little active involvement in county affairs.

On a purely local level, however, Trench was very much aware of his surroundings, of his position in his local community and of that community's position within a regional and a national context. As principal tenant in perpetuity of an absent landlord, his tenancy was secure and his position as senior member of that society unchallenged. His awareness of the different groups within that local society, particularly the poor, led him to comment regularly on their condition, and other writers comment in turn on the Trench family's local aid works. He certainly ensured that all his own tenants were well housed, and his landscaping works employed many people for over twenty years. Apart from that, he had little involvement in any areas outside his own lands and his own tenants, and while he might observe the town and its inhabitants and describe both for Lord Stanhope, he felt little personal responsibility for their development. Rather he saw that as a role for Lord Stanhope to undertake, and he wrote many letters urging him to visit and gently promoted various types of improvements for the town in particular.

In 1770, as a young man of twenty-four, Frederick Trench had visited Lord Stanhope's Swiss home in Geneva where he gave a memorandum of Ballinakill in the Queen's County. From this memorandum it is clear that Stanhope asked for a full description of his Irish property and for suggestions of possible improvements.[8] Trench described the town of Ballinakill in great detail, its economic makeup, how its society was comprised and functioned and of his own position there. The young Trench was clearly aware of and made specific reference to the improving works of the Dublin Society founded in 1731 'for the Encouragement of Husbandry, Manufactures and other Useful Arts', of which he himself was to become a member in 1792. He was also aware of the work of the similar London Society of Arts and Sciences. These eighteenth-century concepts of improvement coloured this memrandum and certainly influenced his many suggestions to Lord Stanhope for bettering the local economy. His analysis and ideas of the society and economy of Ballinakill clearly show that he had a well thought-out and thorough grasp of the local economy, its strengths and weaknesses, the various laws affecting it. He also makes relevant sensible and achievable recommendations for that society's consolidation and improvement on all levels.

At that time the Trench home was right in the town, in a large house with 'garden grounds that joins and surrounds the church'.[9] In 1770 a total of 1,300 inhabitants lived on the Stanhope property of 1,200 acres which centred on the town, although the borough of Ballinakill itself was then owned by the Barrington family. Trench listed those people he considered to be the more important in the Stanhope lands, their occupations and religion. He also listed all the resident gentry and noblemen within a twenty mile radius together with an outline of their incomes, so that 'a just idea may be formed both of the society and the rent most articles would meet with', in other words that society and the local economy.

The Catholic majority 'in the darkest superstition' had a chapel (whose replacement Trench would later oppose). The Quakers had a meeting house and were 'much the most industrious inhabitants, positive and absurd in their principles, but in their conduct decent and sober'. The Protestant minister with four livings had an income of under £600, and the church was 'small and neat, capable of containing more than the inhabitants', clearly implying that the existing congregation could not fill it.

At this time the main industry in Ballinakill was the woollen trade, of which Trench wrote

> the most wealthy purchase the raw materials at several fairs particularly Mullingar, county of Westmeath, and Ballinasloe, county of Galway, each distant upwards of 50 miles; comb and dress it at home, give it out to be spun by the wives and daughters of the neighbouring peasants, and consign the yarn when complete to merchants in Dublin who deal on commission from England.[10]

This industry was dispersed throughout the local countryside, a domestic labour force. Thirty years later, in 1801, Coote noted of the town 'there have been here several manufacturers who were not individually in very extensive trade, but so numerous as to occasion a great home manufacture. The serges and stuffs were sent undressed to Dublin, but the trade has lately much declined'.[11]

In 1770 in a letter to Lord Stanhope Trench suggested enlarging on this industry by establishing a poplin manufacture there,

> to consume the wool when prepared' which would 'centre in the country the principal profit which at present follows the exportation. The neighbourhood from whim, the novelty, or the beauty of the commodity might easily be tempted to adopt them for summer wear; and the refuse or coarse parts by being formed into rugs, rateens etc would find a quick sale among the peasants.[12]

He was clearly aware that the linen industry was spreading rapidly in other parts of the country, and thought that it was 'probable a linen manufacture might be encouraged'; stream banks could be used for bleach greens. 'But as the culture of flax is new in the country, and greatly impoverishes the soil, it would be requisite to support it at the commencement at a considerable expense.'[13] Trench urged that a market be established on a fixed day each fortnight to purchase in by retail the manufacture, would be the most certain method to succour the industrious; a certain immediate return for their labour in ready money must be of vast advantage and some trifling Premium would breed emulation among them.[14]

In 1887 Ballinakill was described as 'one of the few places in Ireland where a weaving industry exists, the work being done by hand-looms', where one tenant had eight hand-looms and a 'good hand could turn out 30 yards in a day, and the coarse flannel, which has more the appearance of sacking than anything else, is sent down to the west, where it is in great request for clothing.'[15] Through his Galway family connections and because of his Mayo and Roscommon lands, Trench was quite familiar with the west of Ireland.

In 1770 Ballinakill was the market town for the barony, holding three fairs in the year (at least one of which continued very successfully into living memory).[16] There were two weekly markets on Wednesday and Saturday. The Saturday market was the bigger market for beef, mutton, veal, corn and coals. The market catchment area included the Durrow area, four miles away, as well as some Castlecomer collieries. Frederick Trench saw that Ballinakill's only hope of prosperity was to build on and increase these markets as 'its only resource is from a numerous neighbourhood, who .. would sooner purchase here than send to a greater distance'. He stated that the 'establishment of a market and securing plenty for all the inhabitants, and manufacturers, ought to be the first case'.[17] He recommended that the resident excise man be obliged to 'a strict execution of his office and preventing his taking bribes' and urged that the clerks of the market, who were responsible for examining meat, corn and bread weights, be supervised as 'an attention in this employ is of very particular advantage to the poor'.

The condition of the poor was always a particular concern of his. In 1774, with a total income from rents of £946.19s.2d., Stanhope's agent, Malachy Delaney, accounted for £3.8s.3d. spent on 'cash paid for badging and cloathing ye poore in Ballynakill',[18] which small sum might indicate relatively few poor in the area or else reluctant or minimal charity. Twenty years later, in 1794, in the expenditure of Trench's Heywood demesne there were several charitable entries: shoes for the poor at 6s.8d., a donation to the poor at 6s.3d., and a gift to Widow Kelly's sons of 11s.4d., schooling for Heyden at 10s.3d. and a bed tick for Kirby at 14s.8d.[19] This total of £2.9s.6d. from one individual makes an interesting comparison with the Stanhope figure of £3.8s.3d. for the poor twenty years earlier. In 1794, the Stanhope agent accounted for no money spent at all on the poor that year.

This concern for the poor, expressed in every aspect of the 1770 memorandum, continued throughout Trench's life. His last series of references to the poor of Ballinakill followed the collapse of agricultural prices after the end of the Napoleonic wars and a series of failures of the potato crop in 1817 and more severely in 1821.[20] By now he was a much older man, and was clearly aware that this community was changing. 'In truth I have very little intercourse with the town or the inhabitants, and in seven weeks since my arrival I have been not twice in the street'.[21] In 1820 he wrote to Lord Stanhope in response to a query about a dispute over tolls;

> The absolute poverty and wretchedness of the place (much worse than usual) would overwhelm you with applications and importunities, painful because impossible to relieve; I am certain of the goodness of your heart, enquire what can be done, you may light on something practicable.

He continued:

> I can safely assure you that for near half a century Mrs T[rench] and my family have ever been active and attentive not only for the poor on your territories, but for those of the surrounding absentees. I much fear we shall all sustain a serious personal inconvenience in our rents; saleable articles are one third and in some instances one half inferior to the prices they bore this corresponding month in 1819. Of this plenty those who have specie may profit, but employment is at a stand. Farmers work day-labour for themselves, banks not discounting random, good credit unless.[22]

This hardship led to the growth of secret societies in Queen's County. In 1821 Trench signed his name to a broadsheet publicising an 1821 meeting in Ballinakill called to address the popular unrest, agitation and consequent 'night meetings' arising out of this depression. This again demonstrated Trench's local concerns and involvement.[23]

This concern for the poor continued. In 1821 he wrote:

> I cannot describe to you the state of our poor here. Potatoes tis true are for one penny per stone; that is fourteen pounds in weight so at present we cannot have a Famine, but all our grain has fallen full one half of its former respective prices.[24] No employment either in Manufacture or work; an absolute scarcity of circulating medium. Few have been so fortunate as you have been in rents, your immediate tenants under the mild government they experience make every effort for punctuality; but the numerous poor, of the lowest description, the under tenants, are wretched in the extreme. We have done and continue to do everything we can for them.[25]

As part of his efforts to relieve this situation, Trench appealed to some of his friends. In a letter of July 1822 from a friend, Reverend King, (who was based at Ely Cathedral and had visited Heywood the previous year), was enclosed a donation for the relief of the 'sick and unemployed in your vicinity and to the diminution of that aggravated pressure as to food which you expect in the month so nearly approaching.' This letter describes the 'daily exercise of benevolence which I witnessed during my very pleasant sojourn at Heywood and which seemed to me to be kept up by yourself and every member of your family from sunrise to sunset.'[26]

In 1758 one in a series of government acts to encourage tillage and thus employment had been passed, grant aiding flour and corn transported by road to Dublin.[27] By giving higher rates for flour than for wheat, this act encouraged investment in new flour mills. In Ballinakill the 1794 Stanhope rental lists a Mr Goss as the tenant at 'the New Mills at Ballinakill'[28] and this is confirmed in 1801 by Coote, 'Near to Ballinakill is another bolting mill, Mr Goss the proprietor'.[29] In 1770 Frederick Trench was not convinced this interference in the market to be for the best of all, as 'country gentlemen find great advantage [and] have almost everywhere erected bolting mills and purchase up and monopolise the grain of the country. Such conduct in a course of time must produce a scarcity among the poor'. Instead he suggested that Lord Stanhope establish a corn market every Wednesday, 'by regulating a medium price, according to the season and crop, between the buyer and seller, and that the farmer may not be disappointed of cash for his corn in failure of other purchasers, let it be bought up by an agent and either resold or transmitted to Dublin, or else a storehouse to be built behind the Market House, where the corn might be deposited in safety for the owner, until an ensuing market'.[30] He considered the bakers were 'as good and as reasonable as could be wished for' but this was not a constant condition as in 1809 he queried the options for regulating the butchers and bakers in Ballinakill again.[31] The 1770 butchers were described as 'wretchedly poor' and Trench suggested that 'any unsold quantities of beef to be purchased at a reasonable rate, salted and disposed of in small pieces to the peasants who would be happy purchasers; thus the loss of stale meat to the butchers would be prevented, slaughtering encouraged, and the labourers better enabled to undergo their fatigue'.[32] He recommended that a public coal yard be established to buy wholesale from the coalmines in the summer when prices were lower and transport easier. 'The poor destitute of money sufficient to advance at a proper season to lay in a stock are sometimes reduced to extremities', and 'by selling out by moderate quantities at a small profit, the poor would find relief in the most severe season', thus producing 'unspeakable advantages'.[33]

As well as these interventionist-based commercial and charitable improvements, Trench also suggested a number of measures to improve the physical and picturesque appearance of Ballinakill town. More in keeping with his own personal interests, these included a steeple and spire for the church, as

9. View from the Dublin Approach to Heywood, in the Queen's Co. Ireland,
The Seat of Frederick Trench Esquire.

well as improving the square with paved footpaths, trees and a fountain, as was
becoming the fashion.[34] He also recommended retaining the by then ruinous
Ballinakill Castle as a 'beautiful object from several points of view'. He
described closely the current laws on tree planting, explaining how, once a
tenant registered new planting with a county clerk, those trees became the
tenant's property.

Trench himself carried out very extensive tree planting on the demesne
over many years. In the spring of 1807 he described his trees in a typical
combination of highly romantic language with his very practical practice, thus:

> [Heywood has] the most singular foliage that ever existed in nature.
> Many of the oak and elms are as rich in green as velvet, but the beeches
> have this early assumed their velvet drapery and the city corporations
> headed by their aldermen are nothing to them. Except some Palace of
> Pluto at some opera I have not even in art seen any attempt to represent
> them. Beech being the predominant planting here gives this very strange
> effect and the heavy hand I laid on them this summer in thinning has
> produced much satisfaction to me.[35]

In 1818 he wrote of 'old and ornamental trees which my grandfather, father
and I have carefully preserved near one hundred years' and stated that in the

year 1777 he had carried out a considerable plantation registered under the act.[36] An undated list – possibly of that same plantation – lists 8,100 trees in a scheme including larch, oak, sweet chestnut, horse chestnut and elm.[37] In the 1770 memorandum he described several options to Lord Stanhope to encourage tree planting, and suggested a premium for planting schemes at field boundaries to 'produce a most pleasing effect' and referred to a similar scheme by the Dublin Society. He also urged Lord Stanhope to build a house for himself on his property and suggested several suitable sites.

Filed with Trench's memorandum is another, a 'memorandum to consider about the best method to do the following things at Ballynakill, if they are thought admissible and to enquire what the charge of each may be, 1770'.[38] This is clearly an analysis by Lord Stanhope of Trench's suggestions, with a note at the end for these questions and orders to be sent to Mr Peele (the agent) together with a copy of Mr Trench's memorial, to be costed out. He queried the sums needed to establish a weekly market for the butchers, for a coal magazine, for the woollen manufactory and its market, for a fountain. He wanted to know what premium would be necessary to encourage planting, and whether it would be advisable to purchase the borough and what sums would be involved. He also noted that the remains of the old castle were not to be damaged. Mr Peele's response to this is unclear, but it is doubtful if any of these – bar the preservation of the castle ruins – were implemented as no house was built for Lord Stanhope, no fountain was erected in the square, nor was anything done to encourage the markets or the industry of the town. As Proudfoot points out, however, where the landowner inherited lengthy leases, as Stanhope did, both their incentive and their opportunity to expend capital was much more limited.[39] So Stanhope's failure to invest here might have been as much from tenurial constraints as any lack of instinct or interest on his part.

Whatever the reason, without support or encouragement from the landowner, Ballinakill began to decline. Neighbouring energetic and improving resident landowners such as the Ormondes and Wandesfords in Castlecomer, the de Vescis in their new town of Abbeyleix and the Flowers in Durrow began to develop their properties and these in turn drew trade away from Ballinakill. In 1820 Trench wrote to Stanhope:

> The new lines of roads lately made have considerably shortened the line from Cork to Dublin, and entirely excluded this town and line of country. Death, the removal of many families and their dealings in new erected shops elsewhere have prejudiced your town considerably, Lord de Vesci, Sir Robert Staples, Mr Allan Walsh, General Pigot, Mr Walker, Mr Doyne, Mr Lyon and several others, who were formerly customers here have for ever vanished.[40]

By the time of Trench's death in 1836, his daughter Mary was to write of Ballinakill to her brother Frederick , '30 years ago its destruction might have been impeded if not prevented by the watchful attention of a resident landlord but all is now gone by irretrievably. Scarcely one enters the town now'.[41] Ballinakill had become a backwater.

On his own Ballinakill property of 258 acres, however, Frederick Trench was very much the master and his subsequent development of these lands matches well with Proudfoot's suggestion that the construction of such demesne parks, subject to the level of disposable income, met the 'double purpose of encoding in the landscape – for peer group assessment – the landowner's cultural values, as well as providing local employment'.[42] With the income from his Mayo and Roscommon lands, he had wealth enough to indulge his passion to create the perfect arcadian landscape on these lands. As well as creating a wonderful private demesne, this enormous project created substantial regular employment in the area for many years and contributed much to the local economy. In a letter to his friend Andrew Caldwell in 1804 he mentioned 'the enormous work of cutting through two hills, no trace of which is now extant'.[43] As well as the tremendous vision, imagination and energy this project called for, it is obvious that the manpower necessary for this work, in a time when all such work was done by hand, before hydraulics and earth moving machinery, must have involved very many men working steadily over many years – a colossal commitment and undertaking.

Work on the demesne was started after his marriage in 1775, beginning with his new house. This was completed before 1789 when it was drawn by James Malton (figure 6). While Trench spent much of each year – at least until the turn of the century – in Dublin in his home in fashionable Palace Row, the entire demesne was completed before 1818 when his son Frederick made a series of drawings of the landscape as it is still today. This programme of works, executed over so many years must have given much regular local employment, adding substantially to the local economy. One letter, undated but clearly in his elderly hand, says that the annual expenditure on the demesne was 'not less than one thousand pounds per annum' and 'to the numerous families of poor who were then in employ it was a regular and secure maintenance'.[44] In 1827 Trench wrote of Heywood, 'My attachment to it has been nearly fatal to me, the sum expended in buildings and ornamental improvements has been upward of £45,000. I state it without vanity or boasting'.[45]

A full account of the expenditure of what was now called Heywood Demesne survives for one year only, the year 1794. Entitled on the cover 'Expenses of Heywood Demesne for one year from 1 Jan 1794 – 1 Jan 1795',[46] this gives the total spent on these works as £1416.7s.3d. for that year alone. This document is most interesting as it is the only annual financial analysis of the work done on the Heywood lands which survives among the Domvile papers and its detailed breakdown of expenditure for the demesne is of particular relevance to the study of the development and construction of the landscape at Heywood. Coincidentally, 1790 saw the end of Frederick Trench's political career – he had been a member of the House of Commons for the borough of Maryborough from 1786 up to 1790, when he was replaced by Samuel Hayes of Avondale, Rathdrum, County Wicklow.[47] It is very possible that this detailed attention to his Heywood estate is one consequence of the ending of his political career and thus may account for the major increase in expenditure on the demesne in 1791.

The 1794 document lists the comparative total estate expenditures for five years in all, from 1790 to 1794 thus:

'to Jany 1791	£925.10.11[48]
1792	1476. 7. 6
1793	1154.14.10
1794	1351.19.10
1795	1416. 7. 3
	£6325. 0. 5'

In itself, this listing out and totalling of these expenses for five years implies that a basic analysis of Heywood expenditure was being undertaken. This concluded that over the five years in question a total of £6,325.0s.5d. was spent on the demesne. In these years, the lowest annual expense incurred was in 1790, at £925.10s.11d. The highest was the year immediately following, 1791, at £1,476.7s.6d. This difference means that expenditure in 1791 increased by 59 per cent on 1790. While expenditure decreased again the following year 1792 to £1,154.14s.10d., as Trench himself said, it remained above £1,000 for the rest of this period. The average yearly expenditure on the demesne over these five years was £1,265.0s.1d. and the year which is analysed in the document, 1794, was second highest at £1,416.7s.3d.

An interesting element in this account is that any monies generated from these Ballinakill lands, whether from rents or from livestock or wool, were returned and spent on the demesne, together with income from either banks or investments, monies coming from outside this property altogether. There is no question of any personal income being drawn by any member of the family from the property, nor any monies being spent on their personal expenses or, indeed, on their house in Dublin. There is no mention of any expenditure on books, furniture or anything decorative for the Heywood house. Rather the property was treated as separate. All rents and other income generated there were reinvested in the demesne, and to meet the costs of the landscaping works, this money was supplemented by other funds generated elsewhere. This could only be done as Frederick Trench and his wife had considerable other disposable incomes, from their marriage settlement and from lands in Mayo, in Roscommon and other property in Queen's County, and so they could afford this luxury, to indulge these landscaping interests in Heywood.

Some perspective on the 1794 expenditure can be reached by a comparison with the rents paid by Frederick Trench to Lord Stanhope for the property. In the 1773 Stanhope rental, Reverend Trench was the first tenant listed, paying £145.13s.0d. for a tenement and lands held in Ballynakill.[49] This was a lease in perpetuity his father Major William Trench had taken in 1728 for 163 acres. In 1743 a further 40 acres had been added and by 1777 the young Frederick Trench had taken up a number of smaller leases for three named lives, giving a total of just under 290 acres in all (see map2). Another document of 1777[50] shows that Frederick Trench had in turn leased out 77 acres of these lands, while retaining 221 for the new demesne. This subletting was bringing in rents of £81.17s.6d., which he was able to set against his own rent of £191.18s.0d. This account has also his earliest use of this word demesne, which is spelt in this document as 'desmêne' in the French style.

In the 1794 rental,[51] the entry for the earlier leases is £175.11s.1d. In addition to this Frederick Trench is listed as having five other lots, a house and lands on the east side of the square in Ballinakill with a rent of £ 12.11s.0d., another premises in Church Street and Stanhope Street at £5.2s.6d., land and premises on the west side of Church Street at £17.4s.0d., land at £14.12s.0d. and 'house offices and part of Glanabrick' at £46.15s.6d. Beside this last entry is a note that this is a new lease granted to Frederick Trench on 3 December 1793 for a 'yearly rent of £46.15s.6d., *which is an increase of £37.6s.11d. per annum* above the former rent of £9.8s.7d.'[52] This note, the only one with any detail underlined in the rental, draws attention to this substantial rent increase, an increase of almost 400 per cent, which in turn implies that Frederick Trench was able to take on new leases for lands he wanted and to afford to pay such a remarkable, substantially increased rent to do so. Thus by 1794 Trench paid a total of £271.16s.1d. in rents to Lord Stanhope for these six different properties.

Although not all of these, particularly the town properties, may have formed part of the demesne lands, the total rents make a useful comparison with the demesne expenditure. Another, perhaps more interesting, perspective on these figures is that Lord Stanhope's total income received from rents for this 1,200 acre Irish estate in 1794 was £1,465,[53] which is just marginally over the expenditure on the Heywood demesne of £1,416.7s.3d. in the same year.

This 1794 demesne expenditure of £1,416.7s.3d. can be broken down into a number of categories as follows: hired labourers, tradesmen (listed in appendix one), materials, house expenses, servants, arrears of rent, shop accounts, assorted rents and sundry small accounts. In the document, the first category has the longer title, 'Task work, hired labourers and horses, sunk fence, planting etc', which gives a more accurate, detailed picture of what it covered. The total cost of this category is £556.9s.9d.

The category of tradesmen includes carpenters, masons, slater, nailers, tailors, thatcher, horseshoer and several others, and totals £247.17s.0d. Materials includes bricks, lime, slates, twine and scollops, dung and so on, and totals £88.6s.0d. The category of house expenses lists such items as coal, hearth money, carmen, letters and malt and comes to £206.9s.10d. Servants appeared to work between the house and its gardens and farm, and two specifically named as gardeners were paid a total of £94.8s.11d. If labourers, tradesmen and materials are taken together, then £893.12s.9d. out of £1,416.7s.3d., or 63 per cent of total expenditure is incurred on works to the demesne in that year alone, a substantial sum by any standards.

If these costs are compared to the prices given for the Queen's County in 1801 by Coote, (for wages and materials just six years later,[54] and also to those more detailed costs given by Tighe for the neighbouring county of Kilkenny for the same year),[55] then a more detailed analysis can be made of this expenditure.[56] By applying this analysis to wages paid, it is possible to arrive at a total number of man-days spent on the estate by both labourers and by skilled tradesmen, to estimate quantities of materials used in this work, and to examine any other entries for which parallels may be found in Tighe's lists, these lists being particularly specific. This in turn can give a closely detailed picture of the tremendous labour, manpower and effort involved in the development of the landscape in the Heywood Demesne in only one year of its development.

The category described in the account of this Heywood expenditure of 'hired labourers and horses, sunk fence, planting etc',[57] has a total of £556.9s.10d. In this first breakdown there are forty-four separate payments listed as having been paid to a total of sixty-six men – no women are listed in this part of the document at all – set out in alphabetical order. Of these, thirty-four payments are to named individuals, and ten are to combinations of named brothers, or entered as '&·son', which is taken as two individuals, or '& brothers' which is taken as three people. This gives a further twenty-two people, a total of sixty-six men in all working as labourers on the demesne. This exercise can be applied to almost all the tradesmen listed out in the account, as both Trench's and Tighe's figures are very detailed and wonderfully comprehensive. Working on the Tighe and Coote figures, an average daily rate for a labourer in 1794 can be taken at 8.5 pence. Based on this rate, these named individuals were employed by Frederick Trench to work as labourers on Heywood Demesne for an average of 174.5 days each in the year 1794. If taken as the flat rate, this really is an enormous labour effort, amounting to just over half the entire year. If a six-day week is assumed, then for just over twenty-nine weeks, or for seven months and one week of that year, there were sixty-six labourers working constantly there. They may also have on occasion worked right through the week, perhaps to finish particular projects, as Trench recommended to a friend to 'dog the workmen and allow them, as I did, a seventh day in the week for extra hours'.[58] This in turn indicates that Trench was willing and could afford to pay a premium rate to complete particular works.

One other way in which Tighe's figures may be applied to this document is to estimate actual quantities of materials used in the construction work. In the expenditure bricks are listed as having cost £26.9s.7d. Working from Tighe's figures, the estimated cost of a hundred bricks in 1794 is 2s.7d. So £26.9s.7d. gives a quantity of 203,700 bricks, which is an impressive quantity to use in a year. Taken further, if this was applied in combination with the days worked by masons, it would be possible to arrive at a theoretical average daily rate for masons, or bricks laid per mason per day. Alternatively, this estimated quantity of bricks may be considered in two ways, either as the equivalent of linear metres of wall, or as possible small tenant cottages.[59] When considering variables such as brick size (taken as modern brick size for the purposes of this exercise), wall thickness,[60] cottage size, wall construction and wall areas,[61] the estimated number of bricks required per cottage might be 37,200. So the quantity of 203,700 bricks could have built at least five such small estate cottages in that one year of 1794.

In all there are 147 separate entries detailing the expenses of Heywood Demesne in the year 1794, and a full list of one hundred and fourteen individual men from that community. All these individual names could be studied further and compared in turn with the Stanhope rentals. This would give a more detailed picture of the position of individuals on both lists and of those who featured only on Trench's list, as this would distinguish between those who were tenants of Stanhope in their own right and those who were subtenants, whether of Frederick Trench or of someone else. It would then be possible (but outside the scope of this study) to build up a picture of virtually all those people, each individually named, who lived in the greater Ballinakill area, the Desertgallen parish, in the year 1794.

One other entry in this 1794 account lists masons as working at 'sunk fence and Daly's', and this might refer to one of two labourer's cottages Frederick Trench described in a later letter as belonging to Daly and 'actually built in my demesne' in the townland of Glenabrick.[62] In 1801 Coote described 'the many cottages through the demesne have all the same appearance of taste without, and bear evident marks of comfort and happiness within to those peasants, so fortunately placed under a master whose kindness is so eminently displayed.'[63] A book of prints of Heywood, undated but signed H. Trench, shows a series of buildings on the demesne. This book includes the gate lodge at the Abbeyleix road, the two gatehouses in Ballinakill together with many other cottages of the demesne as they were originally built. H. Trench may be Frederick's daughter Helena, who is known as an artist under her married name, Helena Compton Domvile.[64] As she married in 1815 these prints would thus be from before that date. They show a series of well-built thatched cottages with latticed windows, surrounded by neat fencing, ornamented with climbing plants. Their smoking chimneys imply fires burning merrily, warming the tenants within. Frederick Trench himself wrote in 1827 'I built 32 cottages at from £56 to £96 each. They give an appearance of comfort not common here'.[65]

As suggested earlier, a detailed analysis of these figures can be applied to give a very full and precise picture of the obviously huge landscaping and demesne development project underway in Heywood. 1794 was only one year in this ongoing development. We know that Frederick Trench began work in 1776 on 'what considerable improvements I have been at all this summer',[66] and was still outside in 1814 'very late and actually dark when I came in from attending the entire day to the workmen'.[67]

The entire demesne of Heywood was all the creation of Frederick Trench (figure 4). His was the vision, the creation, the financing and the overseeing of every detail of the place. He moved hills, dammed rivers, built bridges over new lakes, added follies and garden buildings to highlight the landscape, and viewpoints from which to overlook it all. He named every part of his creation, laid it out and planted it with many trees. He controlled the use of the land, and built suitably appointed homes for those who worked on it. As well as giving the new name 'Heywood' to his demesne, an area and a name that acquired the status of townland in the first Ordnance Survey of 1838 (figure 3), Trench also named very many parts of this land. These names survive in his records, but without maps from his period it is difficult to locate them accurately. Specific names survive only for particular landscape buildings and – with the exception of the seat, called 'Mount Salem Seat' and later 'Claude's Seat' – these are more reliable and can be followed through the various Ordnance Survey maps. They include the Abbeyleix Gate, the Rustic Bridge, the Bath, the Spire, the Temple, and the Moate. Unlocated names for parts of the demesne include Windingate, Lacomon, Grove, Cashire, Wilderness, Bluegate, Lucerne, Roila, and Horney Glen,[68] all of which – like 'Claude's Seat' – are slightly more colourful and romantic in tone. None of these contain any shred of reference to any earlier placenames, but are completely in accord with his making over of this landscape. Lands that were let to tenants however are not given such names and are always referred to in a purely functional way by the tenant's name and their relevant townland.

One important aspect of this world is the relationship between Frederick Trench and those people he employed to work on the demesne. As there is no

10. View from the Window of the Drawing Room at Heywood Queen's Co.
The Seat of Frederick Trench Esquire.

evidence nor any written reference to his ever having had any problems in executing his landscape plans, it must be assumed that there was a willing supply of labour available to him to do the work necessary for these plans, just as he was evidently able to afford it and indeed he paid out large sums to do so. From his work in building houses for his own tenants, described above, even if these may have been built partially to enhance his demesne, and even as a model of benign ownership, he certainly improved the living conditions of those people. One lease from 1801 describes a small area of land outside the Heywood gate piers at the Warren Hill. This area Trench has sublet from Earl Stanhope for five shillings and six pence and now he agreed to lease it to Michael Cahill, provided that Cahill shall 'make up hold and maintain a good and sufficient fence . . . and lay out and occupy said premises . . . in a garden neatly cropped and kept'. Then the rent will be waived.[69] This clearly suggests that the physical appearance and upkeep of a property just outside his gates was so important to Trench that he would willingly waive a rent – however small – to ensure it. A letter of 1827 refers to 'some acres in Castlecoole, where I have built three most excellent cottages and which form a beautiful scene in the grounds', while a note in another hand states that Trench has this

Castlecoole land from Mrs Thompson, who is the listed tenant there.[70] Two things can be inferred from this; one, that this sub-lease was sufficiently long-standing for Trench to consider it secure and to risk building three houses on it; and two, that he took the land regardless of any insecurity, because of its scenic value to his landscape.

Following an 1826 act of parliament to prevent subletting,[71] Trench took care to keep Lord Stanhope informed of changes he was making in his own tenancies, and so there is more information from these years. A letter of 1827 describes how he was 'much against subletting or subdividing land into small portions' and describes how, from 44 acres he leased from Lord Stanhope he had divided 30 acres between two brothers, James and John Campion, and had built 'two capital good houses, with barns and other offices'.[72] Another paper from 1830 stipulates that a tenant has to promise not to burn the ground, and – curiously – to undertake to stop planting or digging potatoes.[73]

Rentals for his lands do not survive for this period, so it is difficult to speculate on any long-term relationship Trench may have had with his tenants, but an account book kept by his daughter Mary Trench (who was to live her life in Heywood) lists approximately forty tenants in 1837, the year after Frederick Trench's death. As these names are familiar from earlier accounts, it can be assumed that these people had also been tenants of Frederick Trench in earlier years. These tenants seem to have paid their rents part in cash and part in goods or labour. This would imply a close relationship between Mary Trench and these tenants, with a mutually agreed flexibility in how these rents would be paid, and in the value of any goods or labour substitutions made.

But for Frederick Trench the main purpose of the Heywood Demesne above all was as a private pleasure ground, an arcadian landscape created to be overlooked, appreciated, walked through and to inspire the viewer. Apart from the lists of trees, very few specific details of the management of this property or of the treatment of the open ground survives. While several documents tantalisingly refer to numbered maps and surveys, none survives. However these documents give some idea of the detailed care that was taken of the property, and indicate some aspects of land use there. One listing of the core 216 acres included three areas described as being in tillage and in joint tillage, but no specific acreages are given.[74] One 1797 survey shows an area in the demesne marked out in strips for meadowing, with a note that it may be useful for yields.[75] Another entitled 'Sundry divisions of demesne' described the south lawn as having 84 acres of 'good pasture and meadow', 5 acres of light pasture and 14 acres of waste, and the north lawn as having 22 productive acres and 7 waste acres. A further tillage division had 46 acres, but there is no indication of its precise location.[76] This reinforces the picture of land most valued for its landscape and amenity use, and with farming restricted to grazing, principally sheep and some cattle, with some tillage.

In 1801 Coote described Ballinakill soil as 'very fertile, and deep clay yielding both dairy and tillage', the pasture is 'rich naturally', and 'throughout the barony they have a well chosen stock of sheep, which is steadily improving', and 'the wool is of excellent quality.'[77] Sheep, being more acceptable to the eye and being cleaner than cattle, were commonly used to graze open areas of grass, and the 1794 demesne account confirms this as it lists £30 received for wool, a further £26 for wool, £3.18s.9d. for lambs and 18s.0d. for culled ewes, a total of £70.16s.9d. in all. The 1818 etchings also show sheep grazing on the land. These would have been enclosed by the 'sunk fence' or ha-ha, the invisible fence so popular at this time. These enclosures were a major element of the 1794 estate expenditure described above. (Incidentally, these sheep may have been cared for by William Flaherty, the herd, who was paid £8.5s.7d. that year and 'Men with lambs' had been paid 6s.6d. in the same year.)

When Arthur Young was in Ireland during this period, between the years 1776 and 1779, he visited a Mr Vicars at Ballynakill who described to Young two systems of sheep farming.[78] Mr Vicars, Young learned, also bought in bullocks in October and fattened them on hay for selling. Cows were bought in May, fattened and sold on in autumn. In Heywood in 1794 a cow was sold for £6.9s.6d., 4s.4d. had been paid 'for the use of a bull' and Mr Ruth the butcher had been paid 7s.4d. Horses were cared for by William Byrne who also worked at the farm and he received £51.15s.11d. that included £14.9s.0d. for oats. Oats and straw cost £53.1s.4d. that year, and George Forestal was paid £23.15s.6d. for shoeing the horses. Potatoes for fowl had cost 13s.9d. These animals may have been cared for in the farmyard and stables behind the house (as shown in the 1838 map), but no details survive of these areas in the papers. Two gardeners were employed at Heywood, Peter Dreelan who earned £8.18s.9d., and Sandy Lawrence who earned £4.17s.5d. In 1807 Trench wrote:

> I never rise without a determination to sit down and read for the day, but the Business of the Farm interfered, I slave till night, never open a book, and rise the ensuing day with the same good intentions, and close the day with similar disappointment, yet this is a point of Rural Happiness.[79]

An undated letter referring to 'old Mr Trench' at Heywood said, 'The house is looking lovely at present, the fresh foliage so refreshing and the house filled with beautiful flowers'.[80]

Whether he is discussing the people who lived in Ballinakill and their concerns with Lord Stanhope, or describing his life among family and friends for his own friend Andrew Caldwell, or detailing his plans and work on his Heywood demesne and for his tenants with others, all these documents illustrate the character, interests and energy of Frederick Trench as he lived out his life. That these were valued and appreciated during his lifetime is borne out by the many warm letters he received from friends of all classes and from visitors to Heywood, all testifying to their esteem for him. The many affectionate references of his children to 'dear father' show this memory continued after his death, as does his grave in Heywood where his memorial reads: 'He was a man of the purest benevolence, the most polished manners and the most refined taste'. In 1801 Coote described him as having

> the most experienced and judicious taste ... in none of the numerous
> elegant improvements is seen any thing of artificial appearance. In each
> of the approaches the most delightful scenes are presented to the eye,
> and the senses of some voluptuaries would indeed be ravished with
> views of such exquisite beauty ... the many cottages thro' the demesne
> have all the same appearance of taste without, and bear evident marks
> of comfort and happiness within, to those peasants, so fortunately placed
> under a master, whose kindness is so eminently displayed ... His elegant
> improvements cannot be seen but with admiration, and to his excellent
> character his whole country bears unanimous testimony.[81]

While his Heywood demesne is now reduced to a narrow core of fifty acres, his refined taste and his restrained style are still clearly evident to the visitor to his romantic landscape today.

The landscape buildings

The piecing together of the estate land and leases, the development and use of the land and the treatment of tenants on the estate have been dealt with in previous chapters. This chapter will look at the different ornamental buildings Frederick Trench built within the demesne itself. Trench designed and arranged these as an integral part of the landscape and they range from the very simple, elegant, classical temple and the seat which were pivotal features in this world, to the more gothic entrance gate, the spire (a memorial to his friend Andrew Caldwell), the rustic arch, the mock ruin and its sham castle, the orangerie, the little grotto-like bathing house, the various bridges which divided the lakes and were in themselves dams, to the final resting place of his family, the mausoleum.

All of this was entirely in keeping with Trench's particular eighteenth-century sensibility and attitude to his demesne. From his house he overlooked his arcadian world, the placid cattle and sheep grazing his fields down to his lakeside, with the whole panorama perfectly highlighted and uplifted by these deliciously sited follies and buildings. Of course all this can be considered as completely artificial:

> Their new arcadias were really poetic lies about their relationship to land and labour, just like the sunken, brick-lined 'ha-ha': the trench that made the garden and the park *seem* continuous while keeping animals off the lawn . . . It was what the English ruling elite liked to think of as freedom.[1]

Inspired by the writing of Alexander Pope and the landscape painting of Nicholas Poussin and Claude Lorraine, these buildings were specifically designed and positioned to enhance the beauty of nature either by evoking a particular association through memory or allegory, or simply by demonstrating man in harmony with nature.[2] Those lines from Pope which Trench had used to describe this world explain this clearly. The fact that some of these buildings were strictly classical and others quite gothic in style did not matter as long as they were kept separate. This is exemplified by the two different views from the drawing room (figures 10 and 11). The south-west view (figure 10) shows that classical, Claudian world with the perfect Temple of the Winds and the seat, while the other view back towards the entrance gate (figure 11) shows the gothic mock ruin, with its window reputedly taken from Aghaboe Abbey, the sham castle and the stylish gothic orangerie.

11. View from the end window of the drawing room at Heywood in the Queen's Co. Ireland. The Seat of Frederick Trench Esquire.

From the documentary evidence available it has not been possible to establish a chronological building sequence, but one can argue that, while the house was competed before 1789, these extensive landscaping works proceeded from 1775 through to 1818, when his son Frederick made the series of etchings which show the completed landscape, as it is still today. I would argue, too, that those more purely classical buildings, (the Temple and the Seat with their clear Claudian idyllic landscape and general Grand Tour influences and as pivotal in the landscape as they are), were the earliest to be built, with the other more gothic buildings following on afterwards. But the whole was completed by 1818.

Howley writes of Heywood:

> Heywood is a perfect example of the best principles of the new gardening, and clearly demonstrates the careful manner in which follies and garden buildings were sited within a landscape, creating not only a good visual rapport with it but also with each other, despite the often quite considerable distances which separate them.[3]

This section will now consider each building in turn. Figure 4 locates each of these buildings in the demesne. Figures 7–11 show them as they appeared to the visitor approaching the house and then as they were seen when viewed from the house.

THE TEMPLE OF THE WINDS

Howley states that 'temples were the only form of garden building to be accepted as serious works of art,' and continues, 'An intact temple suggests continuity with all the triumph of taste and civilisation of the Augustan age, which so inspired the eighteenth-century landscapes of Britain and Ireland'.[4] He suggests that the temple represented a 'symbolic dwelling-place for the gods, an interface between heaven and earth'[5] and the temple at Heywood was entirely in keeping with this. This 'Temple of the Winds' was built on a prominent height on an artificial hill – or perhaps this hill remained while others were removed – overlooking the lakes and fields below, down to the seat and bridges, and back to the house, viewed from which it was perfectly positioned (figures 9 and 10). While only the circular rubble-stone base survives today, from the 1818 etchings it is clear how it originally appeared, a deceptively simple open circular structure with a domed roof supported on eight plain limestone columns.

On the now ruined base is a square stone decorated with classical swags on three sides and bearing the inscription, *Aeolo Ventisq' Sacrum* – sacred to Aeolus and the winds – and entirely in accord with Howley's description.[6] It is commonly accepted that the columns from the temple were re-used in the pergola of Edwin Lutyens' twentieth-century garden at Heywood. Correspondence between Trench and the governors of the Bank of Ireland in 1804 concerning 'ten capitals which were attached to the columns of the late parliament house'[7] has led to the common belief that these are the columns of the temple. But Trench's grateful letter of acceptance refers only to capitals. So it is more likely that these are the four very fine capitals now set into the rear of Lutyens' garden pavilion. Where Trench may have originally used these, and the fate of the remaining six capitals, is unknown.

One undated document in Trench's hand details work to the temple thus:[8]

'Temple repaired	8 barrells lime	6. o·	
	1 do. hair	1. o	
	2 hnd. laths	2. o	
	do. nails	.10	1.1.0
	Burke serving	4. o	
	horse drawing lime	2. o	
	Hutchinson *unclear*	4. o	

These repairs, presumably to the plaster finish with laths, hair and lime, are fascinating as they are clearly just one particular moment in the life of that building, already completed, and for whatever reason needing repair. Perhaps the moist climate had affected the original plaster finish, perhaps someone or something had damaged it. It is tantalising.

MOUNT SALEM SEAT/CLAUDE'S SEAT

Together with the temple, this building is perhaps the purest folly – a monument to a mood – in Heywood. This 'seat' is the other purely classical building in this landscape, and is reminiscent of many other arches depicted in the landscape paintings of Poussin and Claude Lorraine. It consists of a simple classical arch at the lake edge, open on three sides with steps down to the water, presumably so that boating visitors could disembark. It has a simple crenellated top and was originally roofed internally. On the enclosed side the curved back contains a flagged seat, and this is the purpose of the building – as a seat from which the surrounding world could be appreciated. Somewhat overgrown at present, it was designed to be seen from the house, (figures 9 and 10), and overlooked from the temple. It in turn looks back to the house, forward to the temple and out over the expanse of lake water. This is the single building in Heywood which interacts with the lake, itself another artificial feature. The effect was – and is – very calming and evocative of that earlier time.

The seat is named 'Mount Salem Seat' in the first Ordnance Survey map. This is presumably in memory of the house Frederick Trench's father had retired to[9] and it may thus have been dedicated to his father. The name 'Claude's Seat' appears on later maps. This name is much more in keeping with this arcadian landscape and it is presumably a direct reference to the work of the painter Claude Lorraine. The seat was also drawn by one of the Brocas family of artists.[10]

Below and behind the arch are the remains of some other chambers, now in a very ruinous state and difficult to distinguish. One of these, however, seems to have had a low arched roof and to have been decorated with an applied jigsaw of pieces of a rounded naturalistic stone-like substance,[11] suggesting that this may have been some sort of grotto or cave. A grotto, cave or hermitage would have been entirely in keeping in such a landscape, and was designed to inspire feelings of awe and of 'unease in a search for the sublime, in the belief that fear was an important source of aesthetic perception.'[12] This appears to have been a later addition to the seat itself. Other chambers behind this are more similar in construction technique to the Sham Castle (see below) and may have been service areas.

ENTRANCE GATE

This is the principal entrance to Heywood from the original turnpike road. This road ran from Durrow through Ballinakill to Timahoe and divided there for Stradbally and on to Dublin, or to Athy.[13] This was also the road to Maryborough, and at a later date, to Abbeyleix. The gate was the public face of the Trench demesne at a time when image and appearances were of great importance. 'Lodges were not merely garden structures, they were designed as entrances, garden buildings on the perimeter to lure respectable visitors to view similar pleasures within.'[14]

The Heywood entrance is a simple gothic arch between two octagonal towers, one taller than the other (figure 7). The taller tower contained the gatekeeper's accommodation, and had a large bell attached. The whole is crenellated and survives largely unchanged today. A chimney tower has been taken down, the bell is gone, doors have been converted to windows, and a later coat-of-arms has been inserted to the right of the gate, but other than that the tower is as it was built. Malins and Glin[15] say that this entrance gate is similar to that at Charleville Castle, County Offaly. This is interesting as Trench's letters make several references to visits from Lord Charleville, a younger man who began work on his own estate after 1798.

An undated building account referring to the Heywood entrance gate area[16] lists:

> Mason-work Daly
> Arch, Battlement, side wall opposite Gate:
> mortar 4 perches @ 13*d*.   14.1
> facing of sunk fence opposite Gate:
> dry 16 perches   10.0

It is likely that this refers to the arch over the entrance gate and the battlement above, and there is still a stone faced sunk fence, or ha-ha, on the opposite side of the road.

SPIRE

As the visitor entered the Heywood gates and started up the approach to the house, the first object to meet the eye was the obelisk referred to as the spire. Six-sided and made from a pale sandstone, this is quite different from the other buildings in Heywood. It combines two functions. Firstly, it is a milestone, stating distances to Ballinakill, Dublin and Heywood. It is also a memorial to Andrew Caldwell, Frederick Trench's good friend. While it is currently surrounded by trees, an illustration of a contemporary watercolour in Malins and Glin shows it in an open space on the road, with the house clearly visible behind it.[17] An undated letter from Heywood refers to 'a spire at one of the entrance gates which was put up in commemoration of the visit of Mr Caldwell here'.[18] Around the top of the spire the letters TRENCH are spelled out. The side which met the approaching visitor reads

to Heywood
ii
furlongs

To the right of that is:

to
B:nakill
vi
furlongs

To the left, and central to the piece, is the dedication of the spire to Andrew Caldwell. His coat of arms is inscribed first, and then below is the testimonial to their long friendship:

Andreas Caldwell Aim
Dubliniensis
ornamentum hoc
amicitae
qualicuno: testimonium
vosint

The last inscription is positioned to face the visitor leaving Heywood:

to
Dublin
xlvii
miles
by
Kildare

RUSTIC ARCH

My favourite walk, which was my first every morning and last every evening, was from the house to the Abbeyleix Gate – I thought it most exquisite and the most delicious point of it and from which I always felt the greatest difficulty in withdrawing myself was at the Rustic Bridge on the left hand about two thirds of the distance of that gate from the house, when the waster is full (or nearly so) and the landscape is adorned with sheep and the season such as Horace describes.[19]

This gothic arch is a dry bridge, unconnected with any water, but built over an internal road in the demesne. Over it runs a path with low walls on each side. This path is a viewing point in its own right, which leads the walker on over to the upper level of the sham castle. The retaining stone walls on either side of the arch are built in courses to give a banding effect. This bridge exemplifies the care and attention to detail Trench paid to what might seem relatively minor aspects of the grounds. It also exemplifies how he was willing to go to considerable trouble and expense to get the precise effect he required.

SHAM CASTLE AND MOCK RUIN

These are the next features the visitor met on his way towards the house. They are an important element of the landscape, particularly when seen from the house, but they are also eyecatchers and viewing points in their own right. They are built directly across from each other on the road, with the castle giving substance and weight to the gothic window, and so they are treated together here. The gothic mock ruin is constructed as just that – a ruin, a memory of earlier times, positioned in such a way that it frames the view outward, down to the lakes, and is then viewed in turn from the house, ideally from the Drawing Room (figure 11). 'The ruin has all the appearance of gothic antiquity and its view from several partial spots of the demesne has the best possible effect.'[20] Framed by trees, this cut stone window with fine tracery detail together with a smaller window, are long reputed to be from the Dominican Aghaboe Abbey, twelve miles to the west. It is known that the abbey was considerably reduced in the eighteenth century, and later documents attribute this Heywood window as having come from there at that time. An inscribed stone slab has been built into this ruin to further the antique effect, and was transcribed and translated by Canon Carrigan.[21] No reference to this area of the grounds has been found in the Trench papers, however, to either confirm on deny this story.   ·

Behind the gothic ruin lies the sham castle, giving the image of ruins from an earlier time much more substance (figure 11). Built into the hill behind it, this small square building has four circular towers, one at each corner. Like the other buildings at Heywood, it is a restrained building, decorated with simple battlements, arrow slits and a gothic window. The rear of the castle can be approached by the path which runs across the rustic bridge and which led into the building itself, into the room behind the central window. This space could also be entered from the doorway directly across from the ruin, and up a series of cantilevered stone slab stairs (now missing). The views from this height up over the ruin would have been very impressive, looking out over the trees to the lakes and to the temple on the hill beyond.

ORANGERY

This building is unusual in Heywood. It must have been a pleasure building, as were all the other garden buildings, yet is of a more functional construction. Again, it was completed before a print of the demesne in 1818 (figure 11). This inclusion implies that it was considered an equally important feature of the demesne at that time. It is gothic in style, but more delicate in tone than the other buildings. Mainly built of brick, the facade has five pointed arches, the three central arches being larger that the two on the outside. The piers enclosing these openings are finished with cut stone pinnacle and the top is decorated with dressed stone battlements. Internally the building is in a ruinous state, but a series of hollow ducts built into the walls, together with a room thought to be a boiler room at a lower level to the rear, support the suggestion that this stylish building was an orangery or conservatory, and certainly a pleasure building. This building is specifically named as a 'green house' in the first edition of the Ordnance Survey maps, made just a few years after Trench's death. Greenhouse or orangery, the heating technology was the same for both, and Howley agrees that 'certainly, on the evidence of the lithograph, it was at one time regarded as an important garden ornament.'[22]

BATHING HOUSE

This small rectangular building is set into the hill approximately 90 metres below the house. It looks out onto and is a short distance from the first of the series of artificial lakes. The bathing house, and the fountain which was originally below it, were fed by a very strong spring which rises immediately above the bathhouse. (This has been diverted off into a large water tank in this century). There is no trace of the fountain remaining because of this modern work, but the bathing house survives virtually intact. This small building is approached from below by a flagged path which is flanked with large stones set upright in the ground. An oak tree was planted on the left, to partially obscure the building, to make it appear more rustic and natural and in order that the viewer be pleasantly surprised. The bathhouse is built into the hill surrounding it on three sides, leaving only the entrance facade fully visible. The roof is grassed over. The visible exterior of the building is built of the local limestone shale from a nearby quarry, and the wall containing the single arched door and window is also faced with large irregular and grotesque river boulders, to enhance this rustic effect.

The bathing house itself consists of two simple rooms. The door leads directly into a rectilinear room, approximately 2m high, 2.7m wide and 2.3m deep, floored with red clay tiles. This first room was presumably an ante-room or robing chamber, from which an arched opening leads directly to the bathing room. This bathing space, 1.8m high, 3.4m wide by 1.7m deep, is built of roughly cut stone with a barrel-vaulted brick roof. The room consists entirely of a plunge pool. Two steps lead directly into the water, which would originally have been filled from the vigorous spring described above. If the entire spring ran through the house, then the constant outflow may have formed the fountain (described above) before flowing off into the lake. If not, there must have been some system of diverting and channelling the water into the pool, into the fountain, or directly into the lake.

This plunge pool or bath is still filled with water, although this now comes from natural seepage from the surrounding hill. The bath was lit by two hemispherical openings in the gable walls and by an open and unglazed overhead circular roof light, all of which let in natural light. There are also three metal hooks which remain, one in the roof and one on either side of the door to the bath. These were possibly for lamps or lanterns. The bathing house overall is very small and could not comfortably have held more than two or three people. There is no evidence of a fireplace in the building, although a small stove might have been used to provide heat. As this spring water was unheated, a bathe here would have been a very invigorating, almost a medicinal experience.

As described above, when you approach this building you discover it buried into the hill and faced with large irregular boulders. The pathway to the door is between upright flags, waist high, which hold back mounds of earth. The doorway and window are themselves obscured by more boulders, and the whole is screened by strategic tree planting. Taken altogether, this leads the visitor to anticipate a grotto or a cave, both of which feature regularly in romantic landscapes and indeed this is one possible interpretation of this small building. Grottoes, with their classical origins, were considered to hold the secrets of nature. In the eighteenth century, the grotto created an 'atmosphere of gloom, solitude, and shade for the purposes of repose and contemplation, which may in turn provide enlightenment and poetic inspiration'.[23]

There are not many surviving records or examples of romantic bathing houses in Ireland, or indeed in the British Isles as a whole. One reason for this may be that, while the idea is taken from classical Rome, whose bathhouses were masterpieces of construction and engineering, when that concept was translated to late eighteenth-century northern Europe, the experience became much less comfortable and certainly much more spartan. Known examples in this island are at Lucan and Luttrelstown and possibly in Donabate, but it is reasonable to suppose that there were more built at that time. The famous writer and social commentator, Mrs Delaney, who loved both gardens and society, wrote in a letter to her sister in June 1750 of visiting the Luttrelstown bathhouse:

We dined in the cold bath – I mean its antechamber; it was as pleasant as a rainy day could be when we wanted to roam about. The cold bath is as far from their house as Mrs Whyte's is from you; the coach carried us, and brought us back to the house for tea and coffee.[24]

It is not clear from this whether in fact she actually bathed there at all. Her description does imply, however, that it was a social occasion. James Howley points out that this excerpt indicates that garden buildings were used and enjoyed not only on sunny days but also during wet weather.[25] Barbara Jones describes bathhouses as a 'kind of useful folly' and goes on to say that she has

found in accounts of the use of these buildings, no invitations to bathe as there are invitations to take tea or a collation in the towers, or castles; one can only assume that they were either a heat-wave pleasure or a keep-fit pain as swimming pools are today.[26]

FOUNTAIN

This little feature shows on the first Ordnance Survey map as having been sited immediately below the bathing house, and as has already been suggested, utilised the strong natural spring there. A photograph from *Country Life*[27] which featured the Lutyens garden in 1918 shows it as it was originally designed: a classical urn on top of a rectangular stone plinth, with a shell shaped basin below, the whole surrounded by naturalistic stones and ferns. Fortunately all the constituent elements of this feature survive individually, as they were moved (presumably for safety) to the Lutyens part of the grounds by the Salesians.

The urn is made of Coade stone, as is its plinth, which bears the inscription 'Coade, London, 1790'. Coade stone was an imitation stone product, a ceramic product as durable as stone but less expensive.[28] Trench had used it in the decoration of the Rotunda Assembly rooms, and Gandon had used 'compo' for two elaborate decorative panels at Emo Court. The limestone plinth on which the urn stood bears the inscription: *Genio Loci Quieti Sacrum* – 'sacred to the spirit (or memory) of a quiet place'. This is the same romantic sensibility as is exemplified in the temple – that by highlighting and dedicating a place to a particular sentiment or feeling, the viewer is uplifted and filled with appreciation of the moment.

MAUSOLEUM

In a retired solitary shade, with a suitable classic inscription, is erected a fine mausoleum, for Mr Trench's family, amidst the venerable screen of lofty trees, and under cover of a hill.[29]

Maurice Craig describes a mausoleum as 'a funerary structure having the character of a roofed building, and large enough to stand up in, or at least having that appearance.'[30] Although now very overgrown, Heywood has a fine mausoleum. It is slightly removed from the follies and garden buildings but is of that same character, set in a deep valley in the more hilly part of the demesne to the east. Craig says that mausolea are 'stages in the scale by which, according to their means and their ambition, the few seek to set themselves apart from the many, whose dust, almost from the moment of death, becomes and remains anonymous'.[31]

The Heywood mausoleum is a rectangular building, with an semi-circular enclosed area in front, surrounded by a low wall which was originally topped with a railing. This enclosed area was a cemetery, set out by Frederick Trench's father as is explained by the inscription:

COEMITARIUM IN FRONTEM P LX
IN AGR P L III
SIBI ET SUIS COMMUNE FATUM PRAEVENIENS
F T ARM AET XL VI PON CURABIT
EUSEBIUS LEIGHL ET FERNEN EPISCOPUS
SALUTIS ANNO M DCC XC II
RITE SACRAVIT
... SQUE HO ... STULERI ... AUT
IUSSERIT
SUO ... LTIMU ... R
QUOD CUNQUE TETIGIT ORNAVIT
"SI MONUMENTUM QUAERIS
CIRCUMSPICE"
A EM S

The cemetery is 60' to the front, 53' into the field. Forseeing the fate which he and his would likewise suffer, Frederick Trench esq erected it in the 40th year of his age and the 6th of his priesthood. Eusebius, bishop of Leighlin and Ferns, consecrated it in the year 1792. (The next section is unclear) Whatever he touched he adorned. 'If you seek a monument, look around you'.[32]

As Reverend Trench was born in 1715, this dates the cemetery to 1755. He died in 1790 or 1791, which explains the later consecration. This building originally had several inscriptions, many of which are now either unclear or destroyed, but which were noted and translated by the Salesians.[33] Without their work, these would now be lost. They transcribed:

Sacred to the memory of Michael Frederick Trench Esq., born May 1746 died April 1836, and Ann Helena his wife, born August 1741, died July 1831. Their immortal remains are deposited in this spot so dear to their hearts. He was a man of the purest benevolence, the most polished manners, and the most refined taste. This beautiful demesne was entirely of his creation.

Sacred to the memory of Mary Heywood (by marriage Stewart). Her posterity revere her virtues, these grounds not undeservedly retain her name. If worth, benevolence, religion and gentleness of manners avail, she doth not sleep forever.

This urn, a testimony of gratitude not alas an alleviation of grief was placed by an only daughter surviving and most afflicted, to the best of parents who died August 1st 1790 aged 78 years.

There is now no sign of an urn. There are a number of carved panels, originally placed on the wall but now lying on the ground.

OTHER BUILT FEATURES IN THE DEMESNE

There are a number of other features in the demesne which deserve mention.

BRIDGES

Between each lake is a bridge. Each bridge served as a dam to create the lakes themselves, as well as being an ornamental feature in its own right. The fall in water levels caused by these dams gave Frederick Trench the opportunity to create waterfalls, or cascades as they were called, at each drop. The bridge nearest the house is shown in the 1818 etchings (figures 9 and 10) but is thought to have been decorated at a later date with a facing of irregular stones. On the lower side of the bridge are a series of raised ponds, set at the upper water level, from which water cascades over to the lower level below. This is a lovely feature and it is suggested that these ponds would have acted as docking bays for pleasure boats. The next bridge has another cascade effect, as does the one below, although these are not now working as originally designed.

The lowest bridge has a series of chambers open to the lowest lake, which is the one the seat faces. These chambers are built of massive cut stone. One chamber was a boathouse. A second may have been an access to the boathouse from above, giving the effect of the visitor being able to travel by boat – even if by a series of boats – from the top lake down to the lowest one. Just slightly below this bridge is an artificial island built of the same massive stones.

MOTTE

On the upper side of the avenue to the house, set slightly into the hill, is a
small circular earthen structure, marked in later maps as a motte. This may be
the motte referred to in Trench's documents. As the land behind overlooks this
and no other documentary reference to a motte in this location has been
found, it seems unlikely that it is the site of the original motte.[34] It has been
suggested, however, this might just be a large spoil heap, made from the
'enormous work of cutting through two hills, no trace of which now
remains.'[35] All that spoil would have had to go somewhere, and what better
than to turn it into another 'antiquity'.

INSCRIPTIONS

There is another inscribed stone panel, now situated in the Lutyens garden,
which must come from the Trench demesne. With an egg and dart border, it
reads:

> RURA ET BE..CI AUT INIVALLIBUS A..INES
> EI. . . . N.INA AMIII I SYLVAS QUIE

TENANTS' HOUSES

These have been dealt with in the third chapter, and were built by a benev-
olent landlord who wanted everything in his demesne to be appropriately
decorative. The drawing of the gate lodges in the village in Ballinakill
compares well with how those lodges look today.

All of these decorated pieces, buildings, follies, demonstrate Frederick
Trench's 'most refined taste'. He designed and built an exquisite series of
landscape ornaments in a style which, while absolutely typical of his time and
class, was quite restrained and shows 'the most experienced and judicious
taste'.[36] Each piece in its specific detail is entirely appropriate to its location,
and none goes beyond what is essential to that effect or style.

> Nature has been so truly copied by him that in none of the numerous
> elegant improvements is seen any thing of artificial appearance . . . the
> most delightful scenes are presented to the eye, and the senses of some
> voluptuaries would indeed be ravished with views of such exquisite
> beauty. The water, which appears from so many vistas, is all artificial, and
> covered with wild fowl in the season. Several architectural ornaments of
> true classic merit are happily disposed in the most elegant taste . . . such
> a beautiful diversity of the richest scenery, as really produce sensations
> of admiration.[37]

Conclusion

The purpose of this study has been to examine the life, education and interests of Michael Frederick Trench (1746–1836) in order to better comprehend his creation of the particular romantic landscape of Heywood Demesne in Ballinakill, Queen's County, now County Laois. To understand this process it was necessary to firstly look at the general background of that part of Queen's County, the plantation town of Ballinakill, and then to locate the Trench family there. The basis of their family wealth and their relationship with the English owner of those lands, Lord Stanhope, were then considered. This led on to a more detailed examination of the town of Ballinakill in the last quarter of the eighteenth century and to place one particular member of the family, Frederick Trench, in this place, in his time.

The study looked at how Trench developed the Heywood demesne and the way in which an educated gentleman of independent wealth – not a member of the nobility, but because of his interests and education welcomed into like-minded titled society – was affected by the cultural and intellectual fashions of the day and how he endeavoured to impose these ideals on the landscape. This passion was inspired by the interest in the classical world which typified the enlightenment, of which the Grand Tour was a central part. Trench's own very elegant taste and style are manifest in the restraint with which he then used such influences in his building style in Heywood. Having created his physical landscape, moved hills, damned rivers and created lakes, this landscape is then delicately highlighted by his carefully considered placing of rational, classical-inspired elements, such as the very controlled Temple of the Winds and the Seat, pivotal and central to this idyllic image. The study then shows the development towards more romantic landscapes, with their love of mystery and the romance of nature, in the gothic ruins, the sham castle, the grottoesque bathing house.

This study was based largely on two manuscript collections, that of the landowner, Lord Stanhope, now in the Kent Archive Office in Maidstone in England, and that of Frederick Trench and his family, in the National Library of Ireland, in Dublin. In many ways these collections are two sides of one coin, and between them I was able to determine exactly how the Trenches came to Ballinakill, the origins of their money (the accidental death of an older brother being central to this) and how this affected the third generation of this particular family. Independently wealthy, well educated, the young Frederick Trench then turned his energies to his home place. While never owning the lands of the property he named Heywood after his mother-in-law, (which name became set in stone with the arrival of the Ordnance Survey, just after he died). I have examined just how he pieced together the lands he wanted for his demesne and then how he used and developed Heywood. His regret at this lack of outright title to the property is examined, as are his frequent attempts to buy it out from Lord Stanhope. The financing and execution of the entire development has been studied, with a particular focus on the year 1794. Trench's relationships with his local labour force and with his own tenants were also considered. Finally I looked at how his creation was considered by his peers. The research also revealed considerable material on the tenants and sub-tenants of both Trench and Stanhope and on how the town of Ballinakill functioned and then ultimately declined. These are aspects of Heywood and Ballinakill which this study could only touch on briefly.

As this was a highly visual world which was described, drawn and engraved by both his family and by artists of the day, I have also illustrated the study with as many of these contemporary illustrations as it was possible to reproduce here. There are many others, principally in the National Library and National Gallery. The quotation from Pope with which Trench decorated his world, sums up his understanding of his creation of Heywood Demesne, one of the most elegant romantic landscapes in this island:

> To smooth the lawn, to decorate the dale,
> To swell the summit, or to scoop the vale,
> To mark each distance through each opening glade,
> Mass kindred tints or vary shade from shade,
> To bend the arch, to ornament the grot,
> In all – let nature never be forgot.
> Her varied gifts with sparing hand combine,
> Paint as you plant and as you work design.[1]

Appendix 1
Named individuals working in Heywood Demesne in the year 1794

Surname	Firstname	Trade	Surname	Firstname	Trade
Bergin	Patrick	labourer	Fougarty	Edward	labourer
Brennan	Thomas	labourer	Gorman	James	labourer
Brennan	Tim	labourer	Gorman	Martin	labourer
Brophy	Darby	labourer	Gorman	Danial	labourer
Bruton	John	mason	Gorman	Thomas	labourer
Burke	Thomas	labourer	Grace	John & brothers	labourer
Butler	Edward	labourer	Grace	John & sons	carpenter
Byrne	Danial	carpenter	Hancock	Richard	saddler
Byrne	William	taskwork	Hayes	John	labourer
Byrne	William	horsework, etc	Hogan		thatcher
Campion		labourer	King	John	labourer
Casey		thatcher	Kirby	two	labourer
Casey	Michael	labourer	Lawrence	Sandy	gardener
Comerford	Patrick	locksmith	Lynegar		tailor
Corcoran	Michael	labourer	Mackey	Edward	labourer
Costello		pumpbourer	Malone	John & son	labourer
Cullen	Andrew	labourer	McDaniel	Michael	labourer
Dalton	Walter	slater	Mealon	James	labourer
Daly	Charles	mason	Meililly	Patrick	labourer
Day	John	mason	Moran	John	labourer
Deegan	John	labourer	Mullock	Robert	carpenter
Deegan	James	servant	Phelan	James	labourer
Delaney	John	mason	Phelan	Michael	labourer
Delaney	James	mason	Phelan	Thomas of C.H.	labourer
Doolan	Francis	labourer			
Doolan	Patrick	labourer	Phelan	Andrew & son	labourer
Doolan	John	labourer	Phelan	Edward	carpenter
Doolan	Thomas	labourer	Phelan	William	labourer
Dreelan	Peter	gardener	Phelan	Patrick	labourer
Dunne	Terence	labourer	Phelan	Thomas	labourer
Dunne		labourer	Quinn	Kieran	labourer
Edwards		carpenter	Rourke	James	labourer
Eyres	Henry	mason	Ruth		butcher
Fitzgerald	William	labourer	Ruth	Michael	carpenter
Fitzpatrick	Patrick	labourer	Ruth	Martin	nailer
Fitzpatrick	Lawrence	labourer	Ruth	James & son	carpenter
Fitzpatrick		taskwork	Shay	James	labourer
Fitzpatrick	Michael	labourer	Sheale	Patrick	labourer
Flaherty	William	herd	Sheay	Luke	taskwork
Flaherty	Edward	steward	Sutliffe	James	labourer
Flaherty		taskwork	Wall	James	labourer
Flood	Michael	mason	Wall	Michael	labourer
Florrigan	James	labourer	Wallers	Patrick	mason
Forestal	George	horseshoer			surveyor

Notes

ABBREVIATIONS

F.A.O.	Flintshire Archive Office
I.A.A.	Irish Architectural Archive
K.A.O.	Kent Archive Office
K.C.	Kilkenny Castle
N.A.	National Archives
N.G.I.	National Gallery of Ireland
N.L.I.	National Library of Ireland
O.P.W	Office of Public Works

INTRODUCTION

1 Edward Malins and the Knight of Glin, *Lost Demesnes: Irish Landscape Gardening 1660–1845,* (London, 1976), pp 94–96.
2 *ibid,* p. 96.
3 John Feehan, *Laois, an environmental history,* (Stradbally, 1983).
4 Arthur Young, *A tour in Ireland with general observations of the present state of that kingdom,* (London, 1780).
5 Sir Charles Coote, *General view of the agriculture and manufactures of the Queen's County,* (Dublin, 1801).
6 Edward McParland, *James Gandon, Vitruvius Hibernicus,* (London, 1985) and his 'The Wide Streets commissioners: their importance for Dublin architecture in the late 18th-early 19th century', *Quarterly Bulletin of the Irish Georgian Society,* xv, no.1, (Jan.-Mar.1972), pp 1–28.
7 Noreen Casey, 'Architecture and decoration' in Ian Campbell Ross, *Public virtue, public love, the early years of the Dublin Lying-in Hospital the Rotunda* (Dublin 1986), pp 69–94.
8 Thomas Mulvany and James Gandon, *The life of James Gandon,* (Dublin 1846).

BALLINAKILL, QUEEN'S COUNTY AND THE TRENCH FAMILY

1 J. O'Hanlon and E. O'Leary, *History of the Queen's County,* (Dublin 1907), p. 77.
2 James Fleming, 'Heywood Co Leix', Laois County Library local history files.
3 J. O'Hanlon, *Lives of the Irish Saints,* (Dublin, 1870), pp 38–41.
4 O'Hanlon and O'Leary, *Queen's County,* p. 234.
5 ibid, p. 234.
6 John Bradley, 'Urban Archaeology Survey Part VI, County Laois', (Dublin, 1987), p. 13.

7 John Feehan, *Laois: an environmental history,* (Stradbally, 1983), p. 337.
8 Samuel Lewis, *A topographical dictionary of Ireland,* (2 vols, London, 1837) i, p. 109. The castle was rebuilt in 1680 by the Dunnes, but was never inhabited.
9 Bradley, 'Urban archaeology survey' p. 13.
10 N.L.I., Domvile Papers, Ms. 11,368.
11 G.E.C., *The complete peerage of England Scotland Ireland Great Britain and the United Kingdom,* (Stroud, reprint, 1987), v, pp 230–237.
12 K.A.O., Stanhope papers, U1590, E.186/1.
13 N.L.I., Ms.11,347. In these footnotes, Frederick Trench (1746–1836) is referred to as M.F.Trench to distinguish him from his father, Rev. Frederick Trench (1715–1791), and his son, Sir Frederick William Trench.
14 K.A.O., Ms.U1590, E.186/1.
15 *Report from the Select Committee appointed to inquire into the state of the Municipal Corporations in England, Wales, and Ireland, and whether any and what deficits exist in their constitutions, and what measures it may be most expedient to adopt for remedy thereof.* H.C.1833 (344.) xiii.1. p147.
16 Mary Trench to Sir Frederick Trench, May 1836, N.L.I., Ms.11,364.
17 Mr Trench's memorandum of Ballinakill in Queen's County given at Geneva 1770. K.A.O., Ms. U1590 E.186/1.
18 George Taylor and Andrew Skinner, *Maps of the roads of Ireland* (reprint, with intro. by J.H. Andrews, Shannon, 1969, of orig. ed. Dublin, 1783), pp 110, 160.
19 *ibid.* pp 110,160.
20 N.L.I., Ms.11,9107.
21 N.L.I., Ms, 11,368.
22 Irish Land Commission record S.1803. See also Registry of Deeds Dublin no. 21176 between William Trench of Mountrath and Mary Cook widow of Rev. John Trench, and Richard Warburton and Frederick Trench both of Dublin, 20th Jun 1722.

23 Sir Bernard Burke, *A genealogical and heraldic dictionary of the landed gentry of Great Britain and Ireland*, (London, 1858), p. 1227.

24 J. B. Leslie, *Ossory clergy and parishes*, (Enniskillen 1933), pp 78–9.

25 Marriage settlement between Revd. Frederick Trench and Mary Moore, 27 July 1745, N.L.I., Ms. D19, 880–92. That the Trenches and Boyle Moore had already done business together with the earl of Mountrath is confirmed by a deed of 1724, Registry of Deeds no.27685.

26 N.L.I., Ms. D19, 880–92.

27 The lands inherited by Reverend Trench lay in the baronies of Carra, Gallen, Costello and Clanmaurice in County Mayo and in Moyvanna in the barony of Athlone, County Roscommon. While always difficult to collect, in the years between 1816 and 1823 these yielded combined rents of between £3,018 and £4,159. In 1803, Frederick settled the Mayo estates on his son Frederick, who sold them to his brother-in-law, Sir Compton Domvile in 1833 for £60,000, less the £18,000 he had already borrowed from Domvile. N.L.I., Ms.11, 368.

28 K.A.O. Ms.U1590 E186/1.

29 N.L.I., Ms.11,368.

30 Owen Salusbury Brereton to Simon Yorke, Sept. 1763, Flintshire County Record Office, Ms. D/E/1508.

31 K.A.O., Ms.U1590, E186/1.

32 M.F.Trench to Mr Peele, May 6, 1770, K.A.O., U 1590, E186/1.

33 K.A.O., Ms. U1590 E186/1.

34 K.A.O. Ms. U1590 E186/1.

35 K.A.O. Ms.U1590 A45/1.

36 K.A.O., Ms.U1590, A45/1.

37 Kilkenny College Register, Kilkenny.

38 Leslie, *Ossory clergy*, p. 79.

39 Burke, *Landed gentry*, p. 1227.

40 N.L.I., Ms.11,347.

41 M.F. Trench to Lord Stanhope, Mar. 14, 1775, K.A.O., U.1590, E.186/1.

42 Rev. Frederick Trench to M.F. Trench, Jan.14, 1775, N.L.I. Ms11, 347.

43 K.A.O., Ms. U1590, E.186/1.

44 K.A.O., Ms. U1590, E.186/1.

45 McParland, *James Gandon*, pp 121–2.

46 M.F. Trench to Lord Stanhope, June 12, 1827, K.A.O., Ms.U1590, E186/2. He is referring here to lands also in Queen's County, in the townlands of Annagh and Derrynaseeragh, where the house Mount Salem was (see map 2).

47 M.F.Trench to Lord Stanhope, June 12, 1827, K.A.O., Ms.U1590, E186/2.

48 M.F.Trench to Lord Stanhope, July 8, 1827, K.A.O., Ms.U1590, E.186/1.

49 Lord Stanhope to Frederick William Trench, July 19, 1827, K.A.O., Ms.U1590, E186/2.

50 Lord Stanhope to Frederick William Trench, August 14, 1838, K.A.O., Ms.U1590, E186/2.

51 Lord Stanhope to Thomas Vesey, Feb. 6, 1846, K.A.O., Ms.U1590, E192.

52 Lord Stanhope to Lord Mahon, August 19, 1847, K.A.O., Ms.U1590, E192.

53 Lord Stanhope to Mr. Freshfield, May 18, 1848, K.A.O., Ms. U1590, E192.

54 *The Times*, 19 April 1889.

55 Irish Land Commission record, S1803.

FREDERICK TRENCH, HIS INTERESTS AND INFLUENCES

1 Kilkenny College Register, Kilkenny.

2 Leslie, *Ossory clergy*, pp 78–9.

3 N.L.I., Domvile Papers, Ms. 11,848.

4 Leslie, *Ossory clergy*, p. 79.

5 William Mulvany and James Gandon, *The Life of James Gandon, Esq.*, (reprint with intro. by Maurice Craig, Cornmarket Press Limited, London, 1969, of orig. ed. Dublin 1846), pp 39–40.

6 *The Art of Paul Sandby*, (Yale Centre for British Art, 1985), pp 9–12.

7 *ibid*, p. 10.

8 M.F. Trench to Andrew Caldwell, 30 June 1806, private collection (with thanks to Jane Meredith).

9 M.F. Trench to Andrew Caldwell, 1 June 1808, private collection (with thanks to Jane Meredith).

10 Where he had James Gandon design his classical villa Emo Court.

11 Mulvany and Gandon, *Gandon*, pp 39–40.

12 McParland, 'The Wide Streets Commissioners', pp 1–27.

13 G.E.C., *Complete peerage*, v, 235.

14 In 1782 Lord Stanhope promoted setting up a colony of Swiss refugees from Geneva in the proposed town of New Geneva in County Waterford, the supporters for this scheme included Andrew Caldwell. Historical Manuscripts Commission, *6th Report* (1877) app. p. 236.

15 Jeremy Black, *The British abroad, the Grand Tour in the eighteenth century*, (Stroud, 1992), pp 33–37.

16 N.L.I., Ms. 11,357.

17 John Ingamells, *A dictionary of British and Irish travellers in Italy 1701–1800*, (London, 1997) p. 14.

18 N.L.I., Ms11,347.

19 D.Allen to M.F. Trench, 15 Feb.,1772, N.L.I., Ms.11, 347.

20 D. Allan to M.F. Trench, 15 Feb., 1772, N.L.I. Ms.11,347.

21 Ingamells, *Dictionary*, p. 494

22 Black, *British abroad*, p. xvii. He lists the sequin (zecchini) as worth 10s. (i.e. 2 = £1).

23 Rev. F. Trench to M.F. Trench, 14 Jan. 1775, N.L.I., Ms.11,347.

24 Marriage Settlement between M.F.Trench and A.H.Stewart, 4 March 1775. Registry of Deeds, Dublin, no. 203651.

25 Anne Trench to her family, 29 Dec., 1817, N.L.I. Ms. 11,349.

26 N.L.I., Ms 11,368.

27 Sarah Pole to M.F. Trench, Jan.27, 1775, N.L.I., Ms. 11,348.

28 National Gallery of Ireland, *Catalogue of Prints and Drawings*, (Dublin, 1988) nos. 7771–7775.

29 Revd. Frederick Trench to M.F.Trench, Jan. 14, 1775, N.L.I. Ms 11,347.

30 A.H.Trench to Andrew Caldwell, 14 June 1806, private collection (with thanks to Jane Meredith).

31 Revd. Frederick Trench to M.F. Trench, Jan. 14, 1775, N.L.I. Ms.11,347.

32 The townlands of Annagh and Derrynaseera, in the barony of Upperwoods to the west of Queen's County.

33 Revd. Frederick Trench to M.F. Trench, May 24, 1775, N.L.I. Ms 11,347.

34 435 acres are described in N.L.I., Ms.11,848. In Griffith's Valuation of Queen's County in 1850, Rev. S.S. Trench is listed for 172 acres in Derrynaseera and 202 acres which is the entire townland of Annagh.

35 K.A.O., U.1590/E.186/1.

36 Owen Salusbury Brereton to Simon Yorks, Sept. 1763, F.A.O., Ms. D/E/1508.

37 Andrew Wilton and Ilaria Bignamini, *Grand Tour: the lure of Italy in the eighteenth century*, (London, 1996), p. 31.

38 ibid, pp 15–16.

39 John Barrell, *The idea of landscape and the sense of place*, (Cambridge, 1972), p. 5.

40 James Howley, *The follies and garden buildings of Ireland*, (London 1993), p. 4. A fountain in Heywood bears the inscription *Genio Loci Queti Sacrum* or 'sacred to the spirit (or memory) of a quiet place'.

41 Barrell, *Landscape and place*, p. 5.

42 M.F. Trench to Andrew Caldwell, June 28 1804, private collection (with thanks to Jane Meredith).

43 Alexander Pope, '*Epistle to Lord Burlington*'. This inscription was moved during this century to its present location in the Lutyens garden building . Its original location is unknown.

44 M.F. Trench to Lord Stanhope, March 14, 1775, K.A.O., E186/1

45 M.F. Trench to Lord Stanhope, Nov. 6, 1776, N.L.I. Ms.11,348.

46 M.F. Trench to his son, Frederick Trench, Dec. 2, 1814, N.L.I. Ms. 11,348.

47 McParland, *James Gandon*, p. 121.

48 Sir Charles Coote, *Statistical Survey of the Queen's County*, (London, 1801), p. 67.

49 Anne Crookshank and the Knight of Glin, *The watercolours of Ireland,* (London, 1994) p. 98.

50 Coote, *Queen's County*, p. 76.

51 *The Irish Builder*, 15 Dec., 1893.

52 Now the Hugh Lane Gallery of Modern Art.

53 Mulvany and Gandon, *Gandon, A Life*, p. 192.

54 Samuel Watson, *The Gentleman's and Citizen's Almanack*, (Dublin, 1786–91).

55 *Journal of the House of Commons of Ireland*, (19 vols, Dublin, 1796–1800), xi, pp 428, 436.

56 *Journal of the House of Commons of Ireland*, xi, pp 452, 468.

57 *Journal of the House of Commons of Ireland*, xi, pp 447–59.

58 *Journal of the House of Commons of Ireland*, xi, p. 443.

59 Watson, *Almanack*, 1792.

60 De Latocnaye, *A Frenchman's walk through Ireland 1796–7*, (reprint of orig.ed. Belfast, 1984), p. 24.

61 Noreen Casey, 'Architecture and decoration', in Campbell Ross (ed.) 'Public virtue, *public love*, pp 77–95.

62 ibid, p. 82.

63 Part of the fountain there is inscribed 'Coade, London, 1790'.

64 Casey, *Rotunda*, pp 83–84.

65 *Dublin Freeman's Journal*, 29 June-1 July 1786.

66 Mulvany and Gandon, *Gandon, A Life*, p. 93–4.

67 Casey, *Rotunda*, p. 93.

68 F. G. Hall, *The Bank of Ireland 1783–1946*, Dublin 1949, p. 440.

69 ibid, p. 445.

70 ibid, pp 458–9.

71 ibid, p. 459.

72 N.L.I., Ms 11,348.

73 N.L.I., Ms 11,372.

74 McParland, 'Wide Streets Commission', p. 11.

75 see the memorial in Ballinakill town square.

76 C. P. Curran, *The Rotunda Hospital, its architects and craftsmen*, (Dublin, 1945), p. 26.

77 M.F. Trench to Lord Stanhope, Oct. 2, 1803, K.A.O. U1590, E186/1

78 M.F. Trench to Lord Stanhope, August 29, 1819, K.A.O. U1590. E186/2.

79 M.F. Trench to Andrew Caldwell, 1801, private collection (with thanks to Jane Meredith).

80 Mary Trench to Andrew Caldwell, 1803, private collection (with thanks to Jane Meredith).

81 M.F. Trench to Andrew Caldwell, 1806, private collection (with thanks to Jane Meredith).

82 Mary Trench to Andrew Caldwell, 1803, private collection (with thanks to Jane Meredith).

83 M.F. Trench to Andrew Caldwell, 30 June 1806, private collection (with thanks to Jane Meredith).

84 M.F. Trench to Lord Stanhope, August 29, 1819, K.A.O. U1590. E186/2.

85 M.F. Trench to Andrew Caldwell, Oct 1807, private collection (with thanks to Jane Meredith).

86 Anne Crookshank and the Knight of Glin, *The painters of Ireland*, (London,1978), p. 174.

87 M.F. Trench to Lord Stanhope, Sept. 27, 1820. K.A.O., U1590, E.186/2

88 Coote, *Queen's County*, p. 66.

FREDERICK TRENCH IN BALLINAKILL

1 Coote, *Queen's County*, p. 62.

2 Virginia Crossman, *Local government in nineteenth-century Ireland*, (Belfast, 1994), p. 27.

3 Sarah Pole to M.F. Trench, Feb.10, 1777, National Library of Ireland, Domvile papers, Ms.11, 348.

4 Crossman, *Local government*, pp 6–9.

5 His name does not appear in the various lists given in J. O'Hanlon and E.O'Leary, *History of the Queen's County*, (2 vols, reprint, Kilkenny, 1981, of orig.ed. Dublin, 1914) ii, pp 783–793. A cousin of the same name who got the Union title 'Lord Ashdown' is listed. This cousin can cause confusion when looking for Frederick Trench.

6 Samuel Watson, *The Gentleman's and Citizen's Almanack*, (Dublin 1786–90).

7 William Tighe, *Statistical Observations relative to the County of Kilkenny made in the years 1800 & 1801*, (2 vols, reprint, Kilkenny 1998, of orig.ed., Dublin 1802), ii, appendix iv, pp 51–82.

8 K.A.O., Stanhope papers, Ms.U1590 E186/1.

9 K.A.O., Ms.U1590 E186/1.

10 K.A.O., Ms. U1590 E186/1.
11 Coote, *Queen's County*, p. 54.
12 K.A.O., Ms. U1590 E186/1.
13 K.A.O., Ms. U1590 E186/1.
14 K.A.O., Ms. U1590 E186/1.
15 *The Times*, 14 April 1887.
16 Personal communication from M. Phelan, J. Reynolds.
17 K.A.O., Ms. U1590 E186/1.
18 K.A.O., Ms.A45/1.Those poor who qualified for relief were given identifying badges to wear.
19 K.A.O., Ms. U1590 A45/2.
20 Gearóid Ó Tuathaigh, *Ireland Before the Famine, 1798–1848*, (Dublin, 1972), pp 137–9.
21 M.F.Trench to Lord Stanhope, Sept.27, 1820, K.A.O., Ms U1590, E186/2.
22 M.F.Trench to Lord Stanhope, Oct.11, 1820, K.A.O., U1590, E186/2.
23 Feehan, *Laois, an environmental history*, p. 294.
24 This was despite the interventionist efforts of government, through the Corn Laws, to ensure a minimum price for grain.
25 M.F.Trench to Lord Stanhope, Feb.7, 1821, K.A.O., Ms. U1590 E186/2.
26 G. King to M.F.Trench, July 29, 1822, N.L.I., Ms.11,352.
27 J.H.Andrews, 'Land and people, c.1780', in T.W. Moody and W.E.Vaughan (eds), *A new history of Ireland iv, eighteenth-century Ireland 1691–1800*, (Oxford, 1986), pp 247–8.
28 K.A.O., Ms. U1590 A45/2.
29 Coote, *Queen's County*, p. 68. Bolting separates the flour from the bran by bolters, cloth sleeves through which the meal went as it left the stones. As these sleeves were agitated, the flour was sieved out while the bran ran down inside them.
30 K.A.O., Ms. U1590 E186/1.
31 N.L.I., Ms.11,368.
32 K.A.O., Ms. U1590 E186/1.
33 K.A.O., Ms. U1590 E186/1.
34 Andrews, *Land and people*, p. 263.
35 M.F. Trench to Andrew Caldwell, 31 Oct.1807, private collection (with thanks to Jane Meredith).
36 K.A.O., Ms. U1590 E186/1.
37 N.L.I., Ms 11,368.
38 K.A.O., Ms U1590 E186/1.
39 L.J. Proudfoot, 'Property, Society and Improvement, c.1700 to c.1900', in B.J. Graham and L.J. Proudfoot (eds), *An Historical Geography of Ireland*, (London, 1993), p. 229.
40 M.F.Trench to Lord Stanhope, Sept.27, 1820, K.A.O., Ms U1590, E186/2.
41 Mary Trench to F.W.Trench, May 1836, National Library of Ireland, Domvile papers, Ms. 11,364.
42 Proudfoot, 'Property', p. 228.
43 M.F.Trench to Andrew Caldwell, 28 June 1804, with thanks to Jane Meredith.
44 N.L.I., Ms. 11,368.
45 M.F. Trench to Lord Stanhope, June 12, 1827, K.A.O., Ms.U1590, E186/2.
46 National Library of Ireland, Domvile papers, Ms. 11,368.
47 Watson, *Almanack*.
48 Where a halfpenny is listed, these have been rounded up to the next penny.

49 K.A.O., Ms. U1590, A45/1.
50 N.L.I., Ms. 11,368.
51 K.A.O., Ms. U1590, A45/2
52 K.A.O., Ms. U1590, A45/2.
53 K.A.O., Ms. U1590, A45/2.
54 Coote, *Queen's County*, pp 49–58, 195–6.
55 William Tighe, *Statistical observations relative to the County of Kilkenny, made in the years 1800 and 1801*, (2 vols, reprint Kilkenny 1998 of orig.ed. Dublin 1802), ii, pp 493–501.
56 These figures are worked up from the 1790 price + 0.4 (1800 price–1790 price) to arrive at a price for either wages or materials for 1794.This assumes a standard yearly increase over this period.
57 N.L.I., Ms. 11,368.
58 M.F.Trench to Andrew Caldwell, undated, private collection (with thanks to Jane Meredith).
59 With thanks to John Ryan, Nolan Ryan Partnership, Chartered Quantity Surveyors, Kilkenny for supplying the estimated quantities in the following paragraph.
60 500mm external; 215mm internal.
61 50 sq.metres all solid brick.
62 M.F.Trench to Lord Stanhope, Dec. 1827, K.A.O. Ms.U1590, E186/2.
63 Coote, *Queen's County*, p. 66.
64 for an example of her work, see Noel Kissane (ed.), *Treasures from the National Library of Ireland*, (Dublin, 1994), p. 56.
65 M.F. Trench to Lord Stanhope, June 12, 1827, K.A.O., Ms. U1590, E186/1.
66 M.F. Trench to Lord Stanhope, Nov. 6,1776, N.L.I., Ms. 11, 348.
67 M.F.Trench to his son Frederick Trench, Dec.2, 1814, N.L.I., Ms. 11,348.
68 N.L.I., Ms. 11,368.
69 N.L.I., Ms. 11,791.
70 M.F.Trench to Lord Stanhope, July 8 1827, K.A.O., Ms. U1590, E186/2.
71 Ó Tuathaigh, *Ireland Before the Famine*, p. 137.
72 M.F. Trench to Lord Stanhope, Dec. 1827, K.A.O., Ms. U1590, E186/2.
73 N.L.I., Ms.11,368.
74 N.L.I., Ms, 11,368.
75 N.L.I., Ms. 11,368.
76 N.L.I., Ms. 11,368.
77 Coote, *Queen's County*, pp 51–54.
78 Arthur Young, *A tour in Ireland: with general observations on the present state of that kingdom: made in the years 1776, 1777, and 1778 and brought down to the end of 1779*, (London 1780), pp 69–70. The name Vicars does not appear in the Trench papers, nor in Stanhope rentals for 1774 or 1794.
79 M.F.Trench to Andrew Caldwell, Oct.1807, private collection (with thanks to Jane Meredith).
80 Unsigned letter to Mrs Caldwell, undated, private collection (with thanks to Jane Meredith).
81 Coote, p. 66.

THE LANDSCAPE BUILDINGS

1 Simon Schama, *Landscape and memory*, (London 1995), p. 539.

2 James Howley, *The Follies and garden buildings of Ireland*, (London, 1993), p. 4.
3 Howley, *Follies and garden buildings*, p. 113.
4 Howley, *Follies and garden buildings*, p. 136.
5 ibid, p. 137.
6 Aeolus was the demi-god who controlled the winds.
7 N.L.I., Ms 11,348.
8 N.L.I., Ms.11,349
9 see above, p. 33.
10 N.L.I., 1961 (TX) 5. O'Hanlon also refers to a 'Trench's Views of Heywood' as having been engraved by Brocas, but to date this publication is unknown.
11 This might be tufa, regularly men-tioned in con-nection with grottoes. In *Follies and Grottoes*, (London, 1974), Barbara Jones describes tufa as a limestone exotic from near Bath, caused by a layer of calcium being deposited on the limestone around a spring, and sometimes called *Pierre Antidiluvienne*.
12 Howley, *Follies and garden buildings*, p. 39.
13 George Taylor and Andrew Skinner, *Maps of the roads of Ireland*, (reprint, 1969, of orig.ed. Dublin, 1783), p. 160.
14 Howley, *Follies and garden buildings*, p. 71.
15 Edward Malins and the Knight of Glin, *Lost demesnes, Irish landscape gardening, 1660–1845*, (London 1976), p. 94.
16 N.L.I., Ms.11,349.
17 Malins and Glin, *Lost demesnes*, p. 95.
18 Unsigned and undated letter to Mrs Caldwell, private collection, with thanks to Jane Meredith.
19 I. King to M.F.Trench, 27 Jan. 1822, N.L.I., Ms 11,348. This is the same King that later sent money for the poor.

20 Coote, *Statistical Survey*, p. 66.
21 William Carrigan, *The history and antiquities of the diocese of Ossory*, (4 vols, reprint, 1981, of orig.ed. 1905), ii, pp 394–5.
22 Howley, *Follies and garden buildings*, p. 122.
23 Howley, *Follies and garden buildings*, p. 26.
24 ibid, pp 146–7.
25 ibid, pp 146–7.
26 Barbara Jones, *Follies and grottoes*, (London, 1974) p. 221.
27 *Country Life*, Jan.4, 1919, pp 6–22 and Jan 11, 1919, pp 42–47.
28 John Ruch, 'Coade Stone in Ireland' in *Quarterly Bulletin of the Irish Georgian Society*, xiii, no.4, (1970), pp 1–12.
29 Coote, *Statistical Survey*, p. 66.
30 Maurice Craig and Michael Craig, *Mausolea Hibernica*, (Dublin, 1999), p. 4.
31 ibid, pp 17–18.
32 Christopher O'Shea and John Feehan, *Aspects of Local History*, (Pallaskenry, undated), p. 32.
33 ibid, p. 32.
34 There are other moats and mottes in the general area, and a townland north-east of Heywood is called Moate.
35 M.F.Trench to Andrew Caldwell, 28 June 1804, private collection, with thanks to Jane Meredith.
36 Coote, *Statistical Survey*, p. 66.
37 ibid, p. 66.

CONCLUSION

1 Alexander Pope, *An Epistle to Lord Burlington*, (London, 1731).